IMAGES
of America

DURANGO

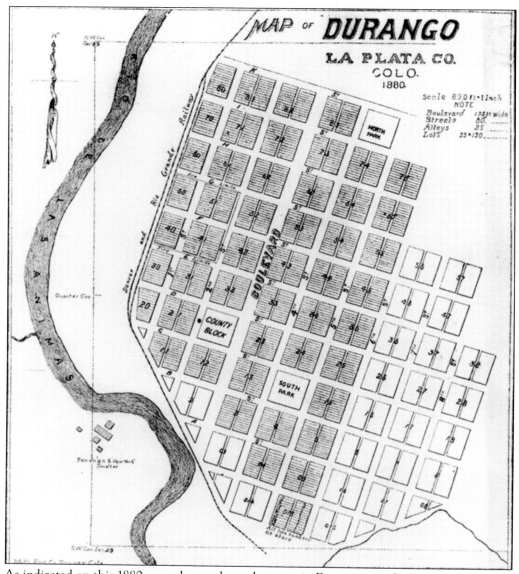

As indicated on this 1880 map, the north-south streets in Durango—with the exception of the "Boulevard"—were originally numbered and the east-west streets designated by letters. Since then, the north-south streets have become avenues. The Boulevard is now Third Avenue. Since then, also, the alphabetized east-west streets have become numbered. D Street (later Sixth Street), however, is now College Drive. (La Plata County Historical Society.)

IMAGES
of America

DURANGO

Frederic B. Wildfang

ARCADIA
PUBLISHING

Published by Arcadia Publishing
Charleston, South Carolina

Printed in the United States of America

Library of Congress Catalog Card Number: 2008933328

For all general information contact Arcadia Publishing at:
Telephone 843-853-2070
Fax 843-853-0044
E-mail sales@arcadiapublishing.com
For customer service and orders:
Toll-Free 1-888-313-2665

Visit us on the Internet at www.arcadiapublishing.com

To my wife, Diane, and son, Kirk.

CONTENTS

Acknowledgments   6

Introduction   7

1.   Ancestral Puebloans and Utes   9

2.   Explorers and Settlers   27

3.   The D&RG Railroad and Durango   39

4.   Early Entrepreneurs   49

5.   The Wars and between the Wars   75

6.   Hollywood of the Rockies   89

7.   Destination Durango   105

8.   The Rochester Hotel   117

ACKNOWLEDGMENTS

My wife, Diane, and I moved here from Lake Havasu City, Arizona, in 1992 after zigzagging up and down the Rockies for three separate summers—looking for a place to relocate, checking out 20 or so towns and cities—and finally settling on the hands-down winner, Durango, Colorado. We were impressed by the spectacular location, the interesting mix of folks, and the fact that Durango is the all-around friendly town it is, where a woman such as my wife can do business.

In 1994, Diane and her son, Kirk Komick, completed the very satisfying work of restoring the Leland House, Rochester Hotel, Wash Patrick House, and T. C. Graden House on East Second Avenue in Durango. As the writer in the family, I did the historical research, resulting in the Rochester Hotel being listed on the National Register of Historical Places.

Some of the images and information in this book are from the following private collections: Jentra Barker, Ruedi Bear, Archie Bodo, Eddie Box Jr., Harry Carey Jr., Pearl Casias, Lloyd Gladson, Tony Herrera, Helen Hoskins, James and Jamie Jackson, Mary Ann Lechner, Effie Monte, Karen Pittman, Tony Schweikle, Duane A. Smith, Suzie Turner Belt, and Nick Zellitti.

Other images appear courtesy of the Library of Congress (LC); Denver Public Library, Western History Collection (DPL); Center of Southwest Studies at Fort Lewis College (CSWS); San Juan County Historical Society (SJCHS); La Plata County Historical Society (LPCHS); and those without credits are provided courtesy of the Leland House/Rochester Hotel. Thanks to Nik Kendziorski at the CSWS and Robert McDaniel at the LPCHS. Special thanks to Robert for fact-checking the book. Also thanks to Andrew Gulliford for writing the introduction and first referring me to Arcadia. Finally, thanks to my computer "techie," Lon Weatherson, and to photographer Chris Giles for the contemporary images.

Secondary sources consulted include *The Utes Must Go!* by Peter R. Decker; *Pioneers of the San Juan Country* by the Sarah Platt Decker Chapter, DAR; *Blue Coats, Red Skins, and Black Gowns* by Robert W. Delaney; *Troweling Through Time* by Florence Lister; *Many More Mountains* by Allen Nossaman; and *A Time for Peace, Durango & Silverton Narrow Gauge, Durango Diary, Durango Diary II*, and *Rocky Mountain Boom Town* by Duane A. Smith.

INTRODUCTION

The comedian and commentator Will Rogers once flew into Durango and landed where Fort Lewis College is now. He later wrote in a New York City newspaper, "Durango is out of the way and proud of it." What was true in the early 1930s is true today. Situated in southwest Colorado at 6,500 feet in elevation, close to the Continental Divide and the largest wilderness area in the state—the Weminuche Wilderness at over 500,000 acres—Durango is one of the few towns in America that is still four hours from an interstate highway.

In 1881, the Denver and Rio Grande Railroad founded the town and built a narrow-gauge railroad up the Animas River Valley, through the Animas Canyon, and north to the boomtown of Silverton at 9,000 feet in elevation. Over a century later, the train still runs, one of the last narrow-gauge steam-engine trains in existence. Hikers, backpackers, and mountain climbers can take the train deep into the heart of the San Juan National Forest, swing off a railcar, cross a bridge, and find themselves in the Weminuche Wilderness and on their way to the 14,000-foot peaks in Chicago Basin in just a couple of hours. When finished hiking, they can return to the tracks, flag down a southbound train, and ride into Durango for a bath, a beer, and a night on the town.

Old West roots of "cowboys and Indians," miners, immigrants, and ladies of the night are still evident in the vital and vibrant Main Street Historic District in Durango, where 19th- and 20th-century commercial architecture can be found—from Richardsonian Romanesque to eclectic Queen Anne to art deco and art moderne.

Add to that the prestigious residential Third Avenue Historic District—with its beautifully restored million-dollar Victorian mansions mixed with simple white clapboard houses with wooden shutters on narrow lots—and Durango becomes an exciting place to live. That's Durango—fun, eclectic, full of the unexpected.

This book by Frederic B. Wildfang captures much of this cultural and social diversity. In his first chapter, for instance, Wildfang discusses the Native American influences in the area. First he writes about Mesa Verde, 36 miles down the road—the world's first park set aside in 1906 to protect not just scenery but its 800-year-old Ancestral Puebloan architecture—and the delicate issues involving the ownership and display of prehistoric Native American artifacts. Then Wildfang goes on to discuss the culture of the Utes, illustrated with many important historic photographs.

What Durango was like in the 19th and early 20th centuries is the central subject of this fine pictorial history. Wildfang has collected some of the earliest and best photographs of Durango, which—unlike many mining towns that in the words of Wallace Stegner "went out like blown matches"—evolved from a businessman's dream to a stable working community. Durango survived because it became a financial and industrial crossroads, because it was at a lower elevation and warmer in the winter than the mining camps it serviced, and because it had quantities of coal essential for smelting ores and running a railroad.

The chapters that appeal to me most are "Hollywood of the Rockies" and "Destination Durango." I enjoyed the photographs of film stars Jimmy Stewart, Marilyn Monroe, Barbara Stanwyck, Ernest Borgnine, Shirley MacLaine, and David Niven—all who made movies in Durango. I grew up watching Western movies. My favorite Western—*Butch Cassidy and the Sundance Kid*, the classic script written by William Goldman—was shot near Durango. Whenever I come up with a new idea, my skeptical wife still quotes to me from the film, "Just keep on thinking, Butch, that's what you're good at." And "Destination Durango" points up the many reasons why Durango has become so popular with visitors and residents alike.

The final chapter on the Rochester demonstrates the dedication and vision Fred, his wife, Diane, and her son, Kirk, possessed in order to take several run-down, dilapidated commercial buildings on Second Avenue and convert them into an office building, a restaurant, and the upscale Leland House and Rochester Hotel beloved of heritage tourists. As a result, Second Avenue has become a delightful place to stay and stroll.

Engaged in the Durango community, a former member of the Fort Lewis College Foundation board, several Center of Southwest Studies committees, the La Plata County Historical Society board, and a juror for the Durango Independent Film Festival, Wildfang writes about local history with the same deep sense of personal dedication.

Wildfang's previous publications with Arcadia include books on Prescott and Lake Havasu City, Arizona, as well as an important book on the Native American, Hispanic, and Anglo heritage of La Plata County, *La Plata: Tri-Cultural Traditions in the Upper San Juan Basin*.

This book is also important. This book is a comprehensive portrayal of Durango as the Old West town it was—grounded in colorful local history—and the New West town it has become—in close proximity to more national parks, national monuments, national forests, and wilderness areas than any other place on earth. Durango has become a true tourist destination for rafters, kayakers, hikers, bikers, jeepers, fishermen, hunters, and other outdoor enthusiasts.

As a former hitchhiking Beat-influenced poet in the mode of Jack Kerouac, Fred Wildfang has made the odd commitment to settle down and research and write about the town he loves. So here's to Fred Wildfang's photograph book on Durango. He has captured the Old West and helped usher in the New West. And three cheers for the town of Durango, itself—between the mountains and the deserts with a steam-engine train and a river running through it.

—Andrew Gulliford

Andrew Gulliford is a photographer, historian, and professor of southwest studies and history at Fort Lewis College in Durango. He is the editor of *Preserving Western History* and the author of *America's Country Schools*; *Boomtown Blues: Colorado Oil Shale*; and *Sacred Objects and Sacred Places: Preserving Tribal Traditions*.

One

ANCESTRAL PUEBLOANS AND UTES

It is thought that Ancestral Puebloans were situated in the Animas Valley centuries before Christ. In 1937, a burial site was discovered at Falls Creek near Durango containing the remains of 19 individuals dating back to the Late Basketmaker II period, 372 AD. Nearby sites, however, disclosed evidence of mud dwellings with walls of logs and storage cists filled with corn. Tree ring analysis of the logs and radiocarbon analysis of the corn—the earliest known corn in the Mesa Verde Province—indicated occupation as far back as 400 BC.

More recent discoveries in the Ridges Basin area south of Durango have uncovered pit houses from the Basketmaker III period, 500–750 AD.

It is possible the Utes may have interacted with the Puebloans before they mysteriously disappeared from the area sometime during the 1300s, though there is no proof of that. The Utes, a Uto-Aztecan speaking people, migrated from present-day Southern California and Nevada to the Great Basin and then to present-day Colorado around 1100 AD. It is known that the Utes were here when the Spanish arrived in the late 1500s. The Utes acquired horses from the Spanish.

With the acquisition of horses, the Utes extended their hunting grounds to the Great Plains, where they were introduced to clothing made from the tanned hides of animals, as well as feather headdresses, beadwork, and teepees.

The Utes established a lively trade with the Spanish, obtaining not only horses from them but also weapons, tools, and blankets in exchange for hides, dried meat, and slaves. As a result of this relationship, the Utes coexisted peacefully with the Spanish, hunting and gathering at will.

After the war between the United States and Mexico in 1848, however, and the arrival of Anglos into areas formerly controlled by the Spanish, the Ute situation radically changed. Ute hunting grounds were quickly appropriated by invading Anglos. Subsequent to retaliations by the Utes, the U.S. government negotiated a series of treaties, restricting the Utes to smaller and smaller reservations. Ultimately, in 1895, the Weeminuche band of Utes in southern Colorado were offered individual allotments of land, which they refused, agreeing instead to move to the western portion of the Southern Ute Reservation centered around Towoac. The Muache band in southern Colorado decided to accept individual allotments of land centered on the independent community of Ignacio.

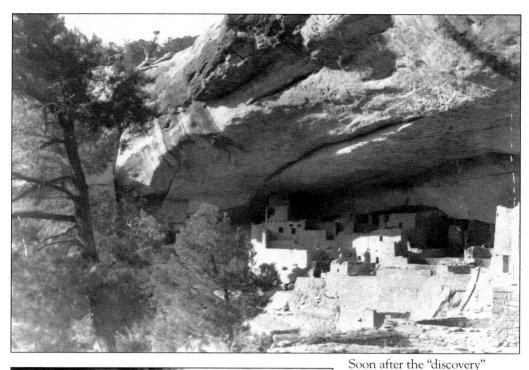

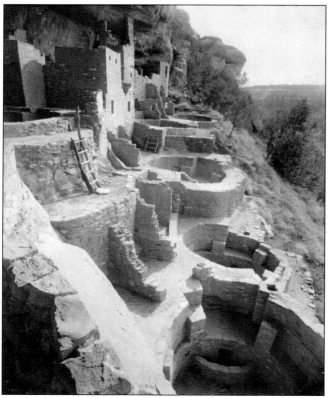

Soon after the "discovery" of the Ancestral Puebloan ruins at Mesa Verde by Richard Wetherill and Charlie Mason in 1888, looting became rampant. Wetherill himself sold hundreds of artifacts to various museums. Swedish archaeologist Gustav Nordenskold was once arrested in Durango when caught with looted goods. Out of a concern to preserve the ruins, Virginia McClurg and Lucy Peabody formed the Colorado Cliff Dwellings Association, which was strongly supported by the Durango Reading Club, a local women's group organized in 1882. In 1904, these ladies tried to lease the cliff dwellings from the Utes, but to no avail. In 1906, however, Pres. Theodore Roosevelt made Mesa Verde a national park. Cliff Palace is shown above in a c. 1911 Pennington Studio image. (CSWS.)

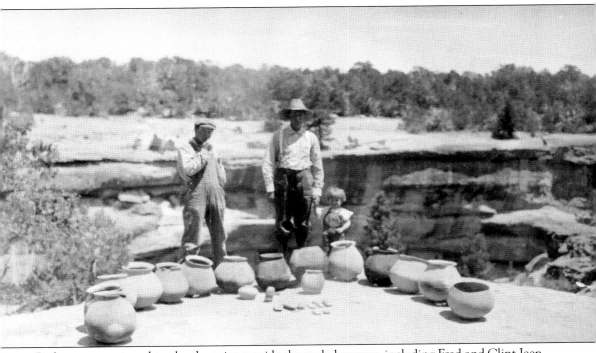

Pothunters continued to plunder ruins outside the park, however, including Fred and Clint Jeep, shown here at Eagle Nest house on the Ute reservation around 1910. One day in 1937, pothunter Zeke Flora unearthed remains of 19 Ancestral Puebloans in a cliff-side burial site at Falls Creek, just north of Durango. Included among the skeletons and relics was one mummified female named "Esther." The unauthorized and illegal ransacking of such burial sites, as well as the tasteless exhibition of their contents ("Esther" was once paraded down Main Avenue in Durango), ultimately resulted in the 1978 Archaeological Resources Protection Act. Consequently, much of the looting and vandalism of Native American ruins was curtailed. In 1990, the passage of the federal Native American Graves Protection and Repatriation Act (NAGPRA) led to the repatriation and reburial of human remains, funereal goods, and sacred objects. (LPCHS.)

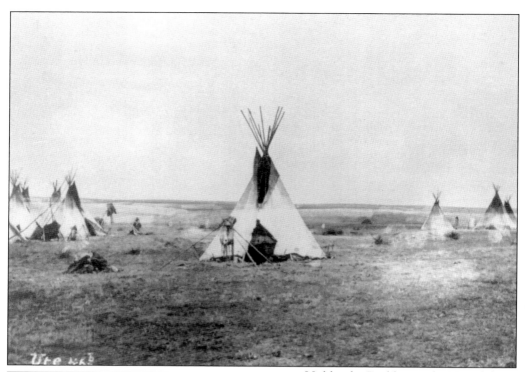

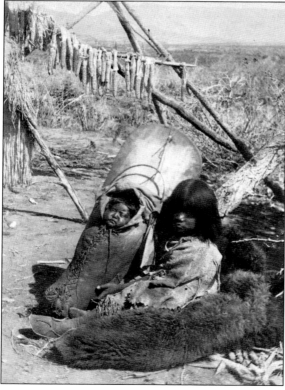

Unlike the Puebloans, the Utes did not build permanent dwellings. Before adopting teepees from the Plains Indians, the Utes lived in brush-covered wickiups. Teepees were able to be transported by horse travois and thus more appropriate for the nomadic lifestyle of the Utes. Before the Utes had horses, their hunting and gathering was limited by what they could obtain on foot. Foods gathered included berries, pinon nuts, roots, wild potatoes and onions, blossoms and fruit from the yucca plant, seeds from the pigweed plant, rice grass, and sunflowers. Once they began to obtain corn from modern Puebloan tribes south of them, the Utes learned how to grow their own. Note the corn drying in the photograph at right, by John K. Hilliers on John Wesley Powell's U.S. survey team, 1870–1880. (Above, Jamie Jackson; left, LC.)

Protein sources consisted of fresh and dried or "jerked" meat—buffalo, venison, elk, antelope, bear, mountain sheep, and wild turkey stalked and hunted with bows and arrows (right)—and rabbits, grouse, quail, and sage hen driven into snares and pits. Fish were caught by using bows and arrows, spears, weirs, and willow nets. Ducks and other waterfowl were caught by using decoys. (LC; photograph by Hilliers.)

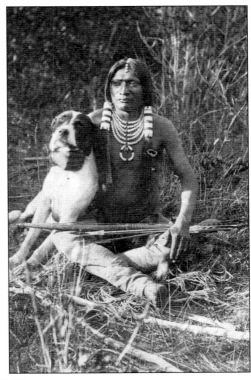

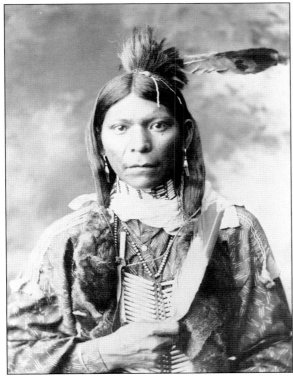

Ute men wore their hair in braids, interwoven with otter or weasel skins at their ends (left, around 1899). Some men tattooed their faces to identify themselves with a specific animal clan. Feathers and headdresses were adopted from the Plains Indians. (LC; photograph by Rose and Hopkins.)

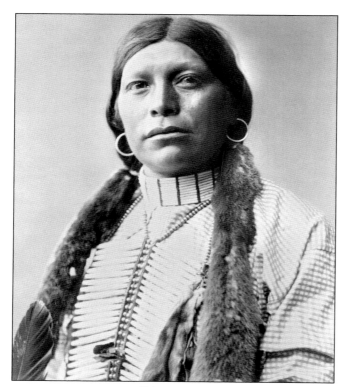

Traditionally Ute men and women wore clothes made from the skins of buffalo, otter, and muskrat, tanned and dyed with colors derived from local plants, minerals, and animal blood. After commencing trade with the Spanish, both men and women wore clothes made from cotton and wool and necklaces made of seeds, bones, and beads (left, around 1899). Utes are still known for their bead and quill work. Traditional floral and geometric designs—notes Effie Monte, famous Ute dollmaker—are inspired by "dreams and whatever they see or hear or the feeling they get from nature. It's carried from the . . . old people, the older generation, grandparents." (LC; photographs by Rose and Hopkins.)

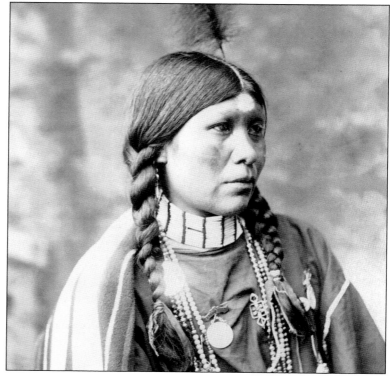

Two or three generations of the same Ute family lived and traveled together as a nuclear unit, headed by the eldest male. The hunting and gathering area dominated by one family was considered sacrosanct from season to season, respected by other families in their band. The five Ute bands in Colorado were associated with specific geographical regions. The Weeminuche, Muache, and Capote bands were associated with southern Colorado. Although the leaders of these bands were male chiefs and sub-chiefs, women in Ute society were well respected. Traditional roles involved child rearing, the fashioning of clothes, and the preparation of food—including the making of pots and baskets for cooking, storing, and hauling food. (LC; photographs by Hilliers.)

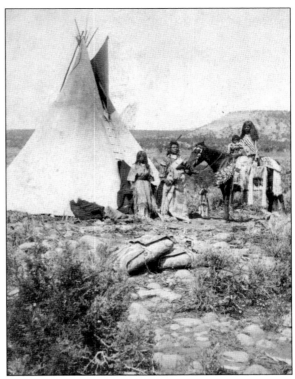

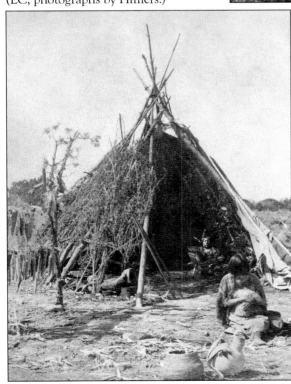

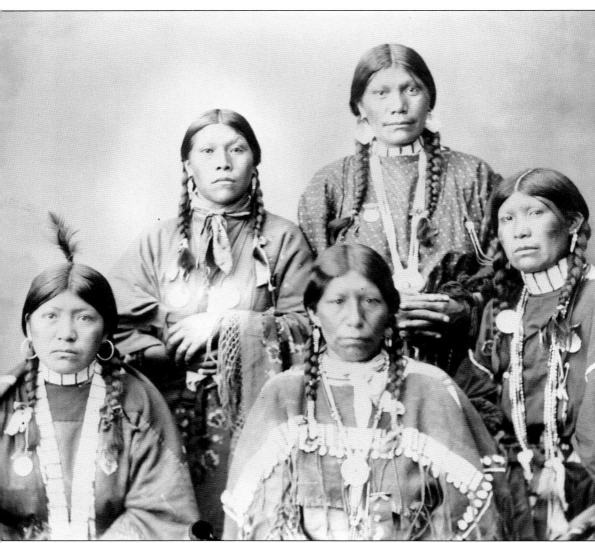

The most critical task women performed was in battle, acting as the front line of offense and defense for warriors on the battlefield. As explained by Pearl Casias, former member of the Southern Ute Tribal Council and chief tribal judge, "When the Southern Ute people went to war, the women marched in front of the warriors . . . [carrying] shields that were two or three thicknesses of animal skins." Women also gathered loot after a battle and took care of the wounded and dead. As Casias continues, "The Ute women had what they called a war society . . . and those that returned . . . those that were not killed during the battle . . . did a mourning dance. . . . And that dance signified an honor dance and an honor song for those warriors that fell on the battlefield." (LC; photograph by Rose and Hopkins.)

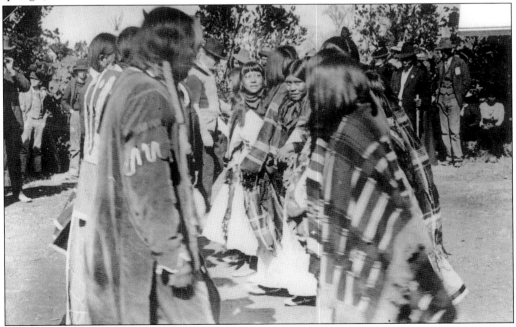

The best known traditional ceremony still performed by the Utes is the Bear Dance, a ritual to welcome the coming of spring. As elaborated by Effie Monte, whose father, Bird Red, was a leader of the Bear Dance, "It was about the renewal of green plants and the birds coming back—and families too—coming out of the winter." Monte says it was also a social dance: "Everybody got together and the families introduced their sons and daughters to each other." In these c. 1918 photographs, women line up during a "choose-your-partner" song and then engage a line of their men in a dance, whereupon the men and women alternately take two steps forward and three steps back, until both lines are moving in unison, imitating the bear when he wakes up in spring. (Helen Hoskins.)

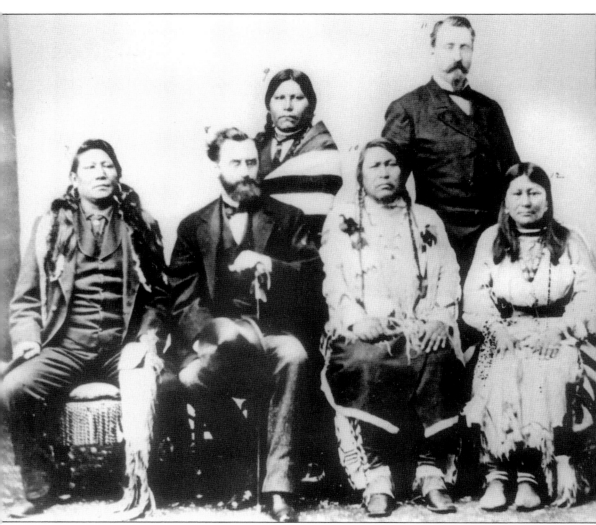

In 1849, the first treaty was negotiated with the Utes, relinquishing control of Muache lands in southern Colorado to the U.S. government, stipulating that the Muache live within unspecified boundaries as well as adopt a sedentary lifestyle based upon farming and "other industrial pursuits" appropriate to Anglo models. Then, in 1864, President Lincoln invited Ute leaders to Washington—including Chief Ouray and his wife, Chipeta (above, first row, third and fourth from left)—to urge the Utes to sell their land east of the Continental Divide and move onto a reservation in western Colorado. Although Ouray consented to these terms, Ouray was not recognized as a representative leader by all the Utes, especially the Muaches and Capotes, who refused to comply with any such agreement. (Helen Hoskins.)

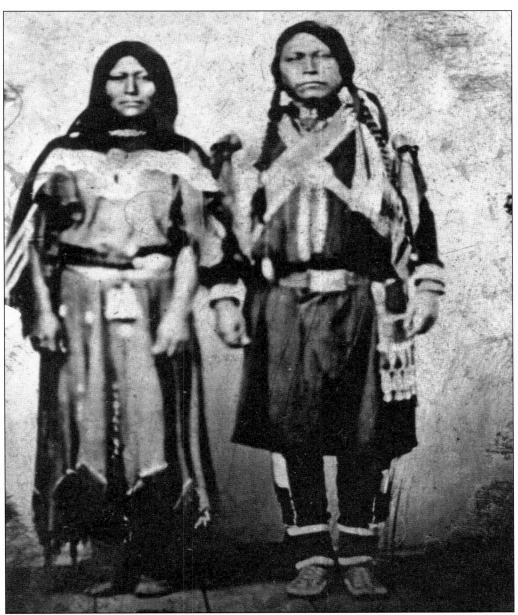

In 1868, the government brought together representatives of the Weeminuche, Muache, and Capote bands and, with the help of Ouray, negotiated another treaty. As part of this deal, the Utes were to receive farming implements, seeds, and food rations, as well as schools and teachers. For his part, Ouray was to receive $1,000 a year for the next 10 years. Southern Utes were greatly disturbed by this whole arrangement, especially with Ouray (pictured here with Chipeta in the 1860s). Shortly before Ouray died, it is said he asked Chipeta to bring him back to the agency along the banks of the Pine River. "He had bags of money, gold and silver coins," as Pearl Casias tells the story. "So he told his wife, 'Take a dipper and dip into these bags—and for each Indian—give him a share.' And so a lot of the people came by and they took that and they threw it into the river. 'Here's your money,' they said." (LPCHS.)

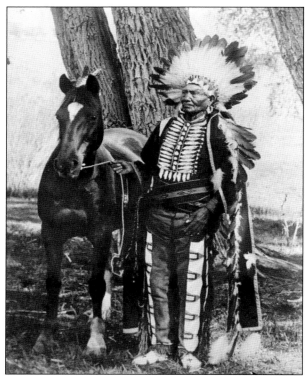

In 1874, the Brunot Agreement ceded much of the San Juan mining district in southern Colorado to the government. As part of all these settlements, the Southern Utes would be provided their own agency and $25,000 per year. Chief Ignacio (left) complained, however, that those payments were never received. Finally, after the Meeker Massacre on September 29, 1879, the northern Utes agreed to "sell" all their lands and move to a reservation in Utah. Then, in 1887, the Dawes Act was passed, making it possible to allot private parcels of land to individual Utes. Ultimately, in 1895, the Weeminuche band, under the leadership of Chief Ignacio, moved to the western half of the Southern Ute Reservation around Towoac, and the Muache band, under Chief Charles Buck (below) took up allotments of land around Ignacio. (Left, LC; below, LPCHS.)

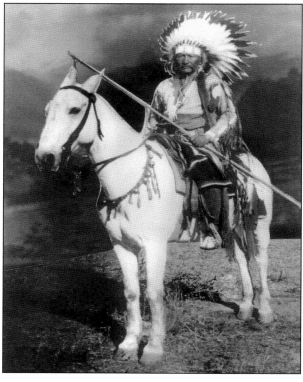

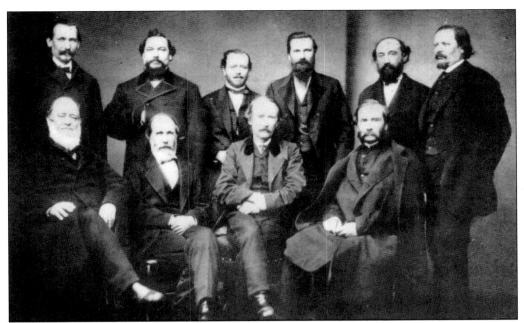

In the late 1860s, Maj. Gen. James H. Carleton (front, fourth from left), commander of the U.S. military in Santa Fe, New Mexico, sent Lt. Edward H. Bergman (rear, at left) to reconnoiter a location for a post in Colorado. Although Bergman visited the site of the first Animas City on that trip, a post named Camp Lewis was eventually garrisoned at Pagosa Springs in 1878. (LC.)

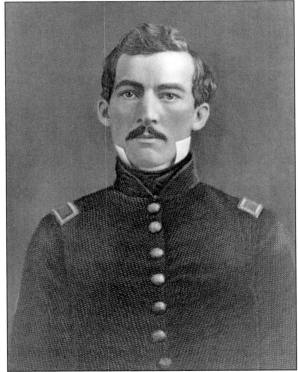

Gen. Philip Sheridan (right), commander of all U.S. forces in the West, came to Animas City in 1879, staying at the Shaw Hotel. Shortly after the Meeker Massacre, troops were sent from Pagosa Springs to occupy Animas City under the command of Col. George P. Buell. Although there were no major skirmishes, some 600 soldiers remained camped on the Animas River, just above the Thirty-second Street bridge, until January 1880. (LC.)

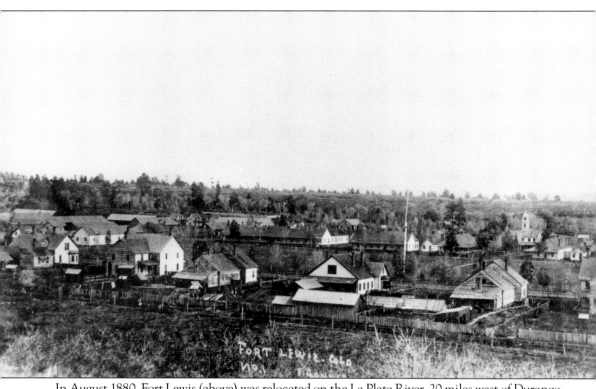

In August 1880, Fort Lewis (above) was relocated on the La Plata River, 20 miles west of Durango, south of Hesperus. In 1891, Fort Lewis was decommissioned as a military post and became an Indian School. As Robert W. Delaney summarizes in *Blue Coats, Red Skins, and Black Gowns*, "No major battles or decisive campaigns had emanated from Fort Lewis, but it had, for a little over a decade, served its purpose keeping the peace. In addition," Delaney continues, "the military post had contributed greatly to the development of farming in the Animas Valley by being the largest customer for and consumer of hay and straw, butter, eggs, meat, and other commodities." (CSWS; photograph by Gonner and Leeka.)

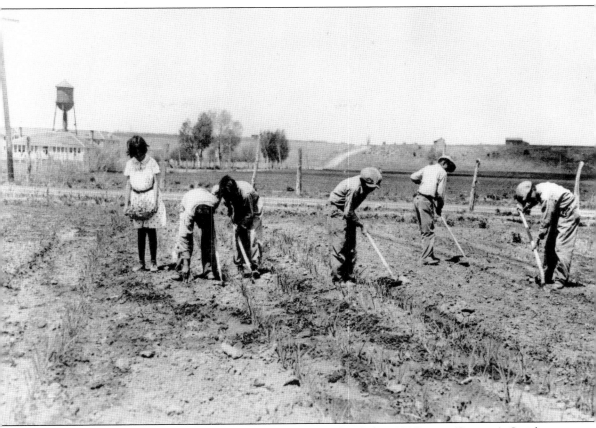

According to the "report of the superintendent of Indian Schools for 1900," writes Duane A. Smith in *Durango Diary II*, teachers "were training the boys 'to be good cattlemen and . . . readily find employment at the stock ranches in the vicinity of the school.' " The objective of the government at Indian Schools was simple, continues Smith: " 'The Indian must be brought to a point where he will feel the work spirit and become self-supporting. Where he will have the ambitions to support his family and not look to the government for help.' " Earlier reformers were more blatant. As Peter R. Decker writes in *The Utes Must Go*, "Merrill E. Gates, the president of Amherst College, believed . . . 'To bring [the Indian] out of savagery into citizenship we must make the Indian more intelligently selfish before we can make him selfishly intelligent. We need to awaken in him wants. . . . Discontent with the teepee and starving rations . . . is needed to get the Indian out of the blanket and into trousers—and trousers with a pocket . . . that aches to be filled with dollars!' " (Helen Hoskins.)

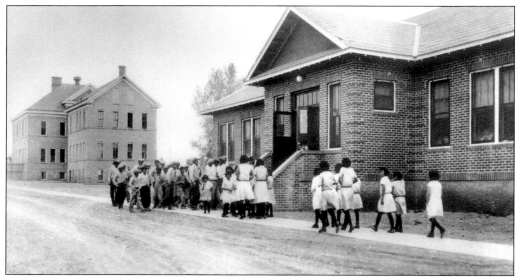

Most Native Americans, however, were forced to go to Bureau of Indian Affairs schools. "The old BIA school . . . was just like a military school," says Pearl Casias. "They got up at a certain time, they marched to school, they marched to dining room, they marched back to the dorm" (above). Also, continues Casias, "I think what the government planned to do was to take the children and place them in government boarding schools so that they would be taught to assimilate with society—and to do away with the culture—do away with the language. I know that . . . they were forbidden to talk their language—and if they did, they had their mouths washed out with lye." Among subjects in the school curriculum other than ranching and farming was learning about baby care (bottom). (Helen Hoskins.)

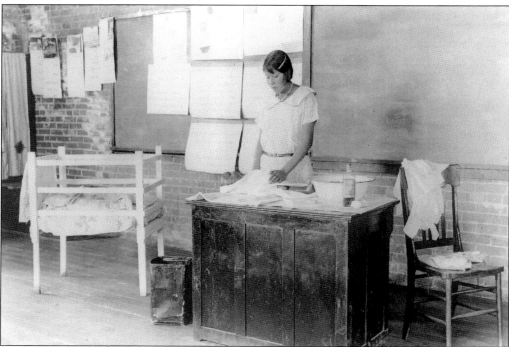

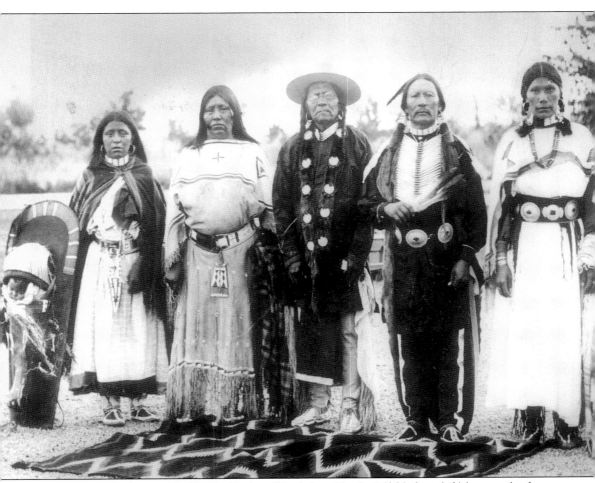

After Ouray's death in 1880, Charles Buck or "Buckskin Charley" (fifth from left) became leader of the Southern Utes. As noted by Eddie Box Jr. (whose great-grandfather, Jacob Bent Box, is pictured here, fourth from left), Buckskin Charley first served as a law enforcement officer, "and that goes to show he had a leadership quality." "He was kind of a diplomat," continues Box. "He would go in there and quiet things down, even when his own people were up and at 'em." Under such leadership, the Southern Utes have become one of the wealthiest tribes in the country. Sitting on one of the largest natural gas fields in the world, the Utes have investments in real estate, energy ventures, and securities amounting to more than $1.45 billion. "I'm kind of grateful for the way things turned out," says Box. "There was time when the . . . government . . . wanted to send all the Utes up to Utah . . . and some went up there, but we stayed. I am a part of those who stayed . . . and I'm kind of grateful for that." (Helen Hoskins.)

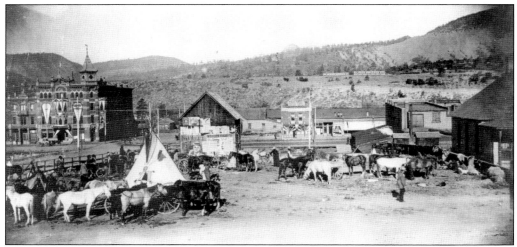

In time, Anglos in Durango began to appreciate the Utes, especially in terms of the trade they brought in. A favorite tourist attraction, the Utes were invited to participate in the annual fair, camping at the fairgrounds or the public corral area in town (top c. 1894 photograph). Buckskin Charley (bottom) often led the parade. Eddie Box Jr. remembers, "We used to bring our teepees. . . . It was fun because we all got to . . . walk downtown and go to the carnival. . . . They would block off the street and we would dance traditional dances." And Effie Monte remembers, "We'd go on . . . horse and wagon. . . . And we used to camp there . . . on the east side of the fairgrounds and then they moved us . . . because many of the other Indian tribes were coming in, the Navajos and the Apaches." (Above, Duane A. Smith; below, LPCHS.)

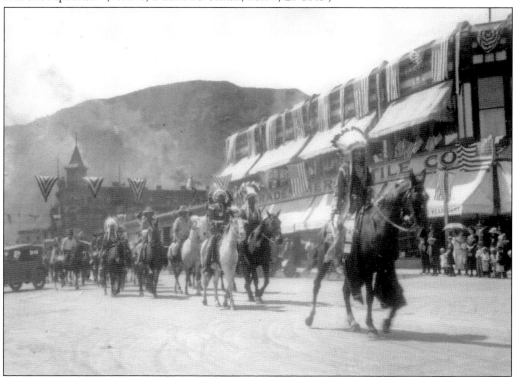

Two

EXPLORERS AND SETTLERS

According to the writings of Juan Maria de Rivera—who came here from Santa Fe, New Mexico, looking for gold in 1765—some of the Spanish place names in the area were already in use. Certainly, though, Rivera was responsible for naming La Plata and San Juan Rivers. In 1776, Fathers Francisco Atanasio Dominguez and Silvestre Velez de Escalante, who came here looking for a route to California, confirmed some of these place names—La Plata Mountains (Mountains of Silver), Piedra River (River of Rock), Los Pinos River (River of the Pines), Florida River (River of Flowers), Dolores River (River of Our Lady of Sorrows), and Rio de las Animas (River of Souls) among them.

Although Dominguez and Escalante failed to finish their trip to California, what became known as the "Old Spanish Trail"—stretching from Santa Fe to Los Angeles—was established in 1829 and remained in use until 1848. The main branch of the trail—passing through present-day Durango via Ute Pass, down Florida Road, and intersecting with the Animas River at Thirty-second Street—was the route followed in 1860–1861 by Charles Baker and most of the first prospectors headed high up into the San Juans as far north as Baker's Park or what is now Silverton, Colorado.

Many of the earliest residents of Durango came down the Animas from Silverton, first stopping near the site of "Baker's Bridge," also known as "Animas City (I)," or at the town located at the site of that first crossing at Thirty-second Street, "Animas City (II)." Among those pioneers associated with Animas City (I), which lasted just two years, 1860–1861, was an original member of the Baker party, John Charles Turner, the scion of a prominent banking family in Durango. Daniel Sylvester Rodgers, also a member of the Baker party, ended up settling in Durango in 1887. Among those associated with Animas City (II), founded in 1876, were such Durango notables as Peter Fassbinder, who homesteaded land now surrounding Fassbinder Park; Thomas C. Graden, owner of the Graden Flour Mill and Graden Mercantile Company; Thomas D. Burns, developer of the Trimble Hot Springs resort north of Durango and the founder of Burns Bank; Charles and William Nagelin, who later owned and operated a blacksmith shop in Durango; and William E. Parsons, who became the first city clerk in Durango.

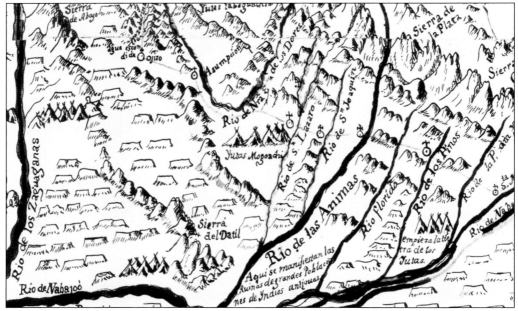

The path followed by Dominguez and Escalante on their expedition of 1776 is indicated on the map above by a series of circles surmounted by crosses, drawn by mapmaker Don Bernardo Miera y Pacheco in 1778. The largest tributary of the "Rio de Nabahoo" on this map—the river now known as the San Juan—was crossed by Dominguez and Escalante on August 8, 1776. The name of that tributary, as recorded in Escalante's diary, was the Rio de las Animas, the River of Souls. No one knows for sure where that crossing of the Animas actually took place, but judging from the map, it looks to be just a few miles south of Durango. Today a monument on the lower Animas (below) marks the occasion. (CSWS.)

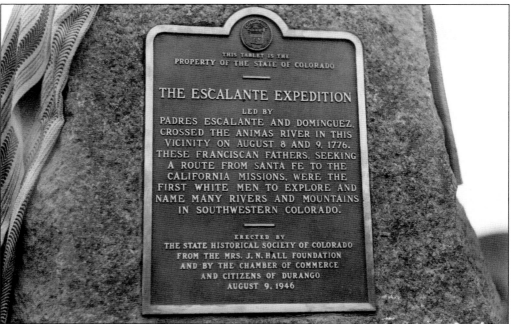

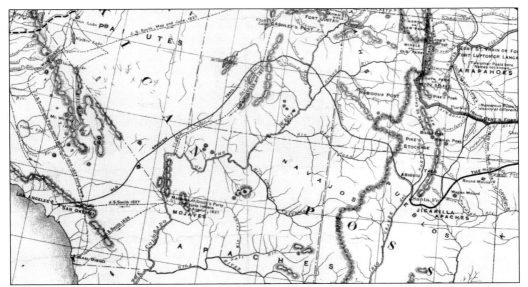

The Old Spanish Trail, as indicated on this map, passed through Abiquiu, New Mexico, over the Continental Divide to the San Juan River and its tributaries, including the Animas River, and then on to the Dolores River. Santa Fe trader Antonio Armijo was the first to make commercial use of the Old Spanish Trail, leading a party of 60 men and 100 mules to California in 1829. (CSWS.)

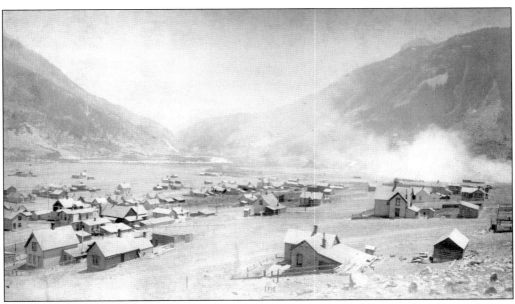

The earliest settlers first came here while journeying to or from "Baker's Park," what is now Silverton (above in the 1890s). The purported original route from the Animas Valley north proceeded overland to present-day Needles, then up Cascade Creek, around Jura Knob, and down South Mineral Creek. Later the route cut down to the Animas River from Needles, thereafter following the eventual path of the railroad to Silverton. (DPL.)

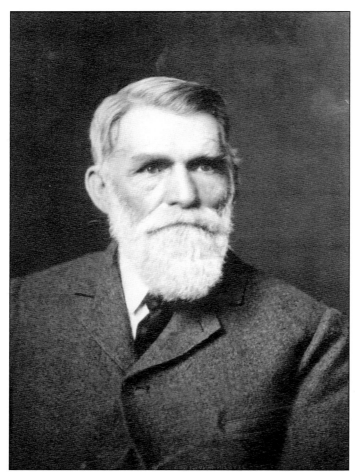

John Charles Turner (left) came to the Animas Valley with the Baker party in March 1861, camping at the first Animas City, near the site of Baker's Bridge. Pictured here during the dedication of the modern bridge in 1930 are (below, from left to right) J. C. Turner's grandson, Richard William Turner Sr.; his great-grandson, Richard William Turner Jr.; and his son John William Turner. After serving with the 1st Colorado Cavalry under Col. J. M. Chivington during the Civil War, J. C. Turner subsequently settled in Colfax County, New Mexico, where he married Emma Sarah Stevens in 1871 and served as sheriff in 1874 and 1875. In 1876, recalling his experiences with Baker, Turner homesteaded a 160-acre parcel on the east side of the Animas Valley some 10 miles south of Baker's Bridge. (Suzie Turner Belt.)

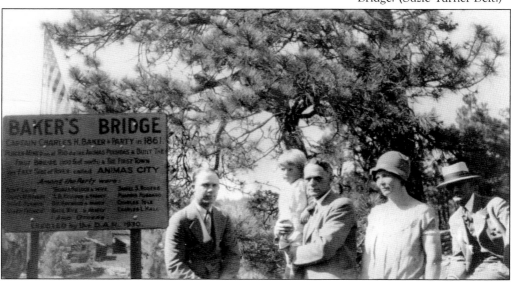

Emma Turner (right) reared eight children on their ranch—including (from left to right) Arthur, Billy, Guy, and (below) John William Turner—and lived there until her death in 1894. After Emma's death, J. C. married Fannie Kavanaugh and continued ranching until his death in 1902. Not only was J. C. a successful rancher in the community, he was also active in local politics, serving two terms each as county commissioner and sheriff. After J. C.'s death, J. W. Turner took over the ranch and helped with the raising of his younger siblings. Eventually J. W. moved to Durango and established the Durango Real Estate Company, which later became the Turner Investment Company, one of the oldest businesses in town. Ultimately J. W. became president of the Turner Industrial Bank, joined by his son Richard W. Turner Sr. and grandson Richard W. Turner Jr. (Suzie Turner Belt.)

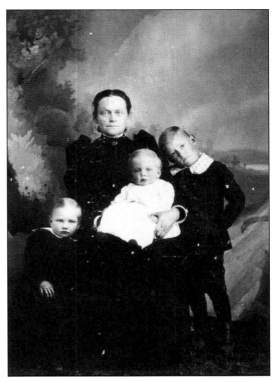

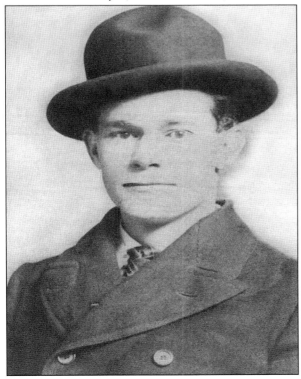

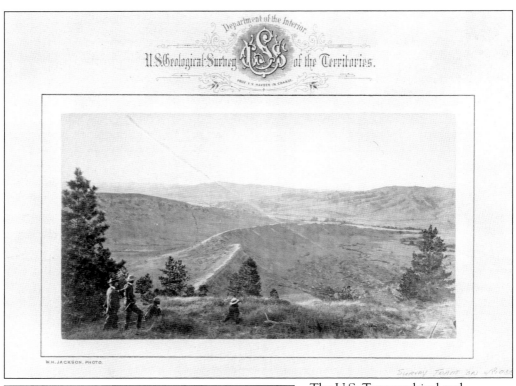

Department of the Interior.

U.S.Geological Survey of the Territories.

PROF. F. V. HAYDEN IN CHARGE

W. H. JACKSON, PHOTO.

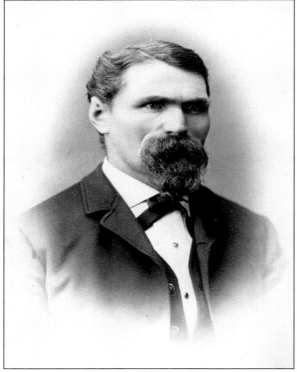

The U.S. Topographical and Geological Survey party (pictured above in this William Henry Jackson photograph dated to 1870–1880), led by Prof. F. V. Hayden, passed through what was left of the first Animas City in 1874. Despite the fact that the town had been abandoned since 1861, the residencies of Tom Pollock, Doc Arnold, Seth Sackett, and Manuel Armijo were found to be still reasonably intact. (DPL.)

In 1876, the second Animas City was staked out on the 640-acre homestead of John Fowler, where Thirty-second Street now intersects with the Animas River. Thereafter, it was intended to extend on both sides of the river—south to the homestead of Robert Dyer (left) at the confluence of Junction Creek and the river and north to the homestead of Robert Lamb across the road from the Waterfall Ranch. (LPCHS.)

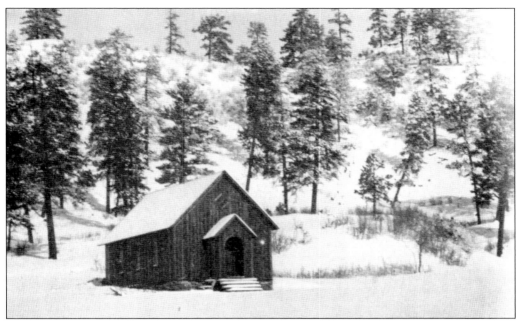

In 1877, famous itinerant preacher Rev. George Darley built the Presbyterian church (above) in the new Animas City, the first church on the Western Slope. Darley organized the Presbyterians and conducted a Sunday school at the church until Rev. W. C. Beebe arrived in 1888. Beebe conducted regular services at the church until 1887, even after the new Presbyterian church was built in Durango. (LPCHS.)

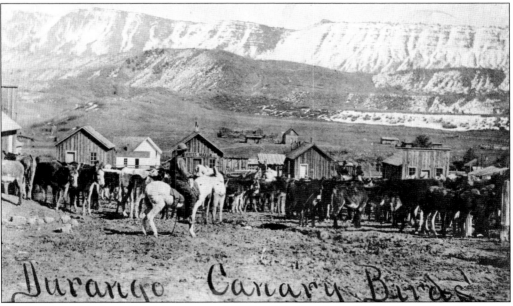

The founders of Animas City (above, around 1879)—J. D. Anenkeny, Ruel L. Nute, Hemel Schwenk, Ira Smith, William Earl, and Canfield Marsh—formed the Animas City Townsite Company, which was able to sell 32 shares of stock at $100 per share and become debt free and incorporated in two years. (LPCHS.)

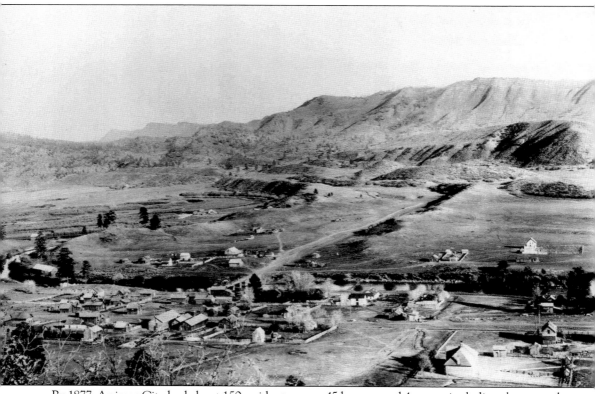

By 1877, Animas City had about 150 residents, some 45 houses, and 4 stores, including the general merchandise businesses owned by E. H. Cooper and Company and Daniel Culver. On May 24, 1887, Animas City also had an official post office. John M. Trew was the first postmaster and town clerk. C. W. Blackmer was the first attorney. By 1880, Animas City boasted some 286 residents and a number of thriving businesses, including T. C. Graden's lumber dealership, Schwenk and Will's saloon, and John W. Shaw's hotel. (CSWS.)

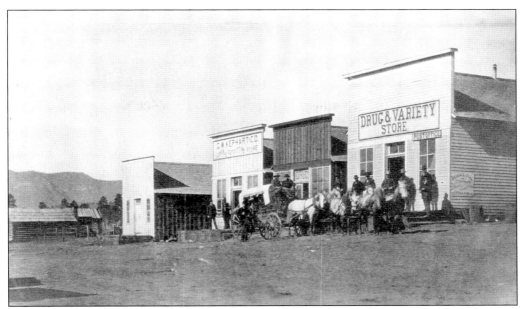

Dr. J. P. Wallace, the town's first doctor, set up a practice in his Drug and Variety Store, also the location of the first post office in Animas City (above, at right). Before A. P. Camp and John McNeil moved their bank to Animas City from Del Norte, George W. Kephart conducted all the banking business at his general store there (center). (DPL.)

In 1881, however, with the arrival of the Denver and Rio Grande Railroad, Kephart and other businesses moved to the new town of Durango, just downriver from Animas City. Animas City remained independent until it finally merged with Durango in 1948. Note the Animas City School, the three-story stone building in this photograph (center). (CSWS; photograph by W. R. Rowland.)

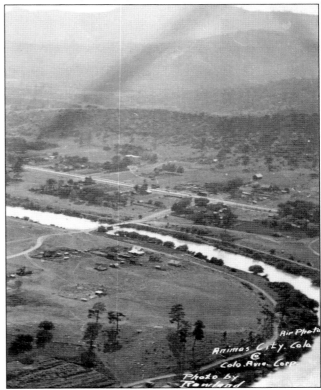

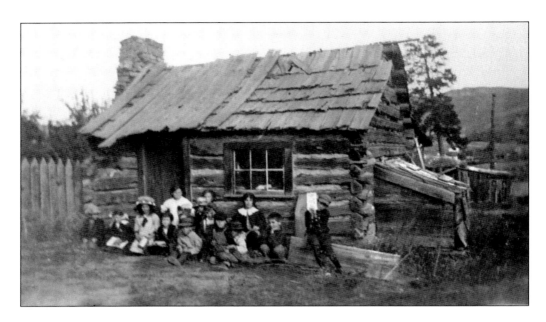

In 1876, children in Animas City first attended school in this cabin (above) and then, in 1880, moved to a new brick schoolhouse on the corner of Thirty-first Street and West Second Avenue. In 1904–1905, the Animas City Schoolhouse, which is still standing today, was built across the street. After a fire at the school in 1919, a flat roof replaced the original hip roof shown below in 1908. In 1939, the Animas City Schoolhouse became part of the Durango school system and continued in operation until 1967. Since 1978, the old schoolhouse—now with the hip roof restored—has been the site of the Animas Museum and headquarters for the La Plata County Historical Society. Historical photographs and archives can be accessed here, as well as exhibits on local history and a tour of one of the original classrooms. (LPCHS.)

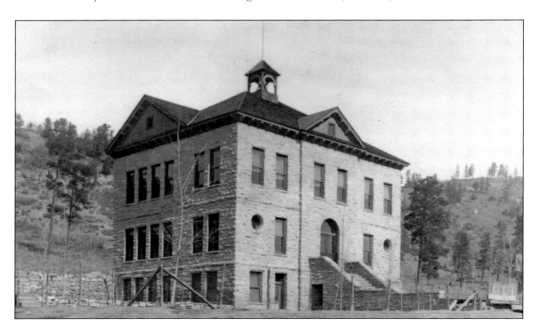

Peter Fassbinder (right) and his wife, Kathrine (below), came to the second Animas City via Silverton and Rico in 1878. Fassbinder homesteaded property on the Animas River, built the first bridge across the river, and provided fresh water for the new town of Durango from the spring on his ranch, located where the fish hatchery is now. According to local records, "Fassbinder took up 160 acres . . . on the north" shortly after the city was laid out and "immediately subdivided it as an addition to Durango." The "Fassbinder Addition" was actually filed on April 28, 1882. Later Fassbinder generously donated some of his land to the city for a city park, to the Catholic Church for the St. Columbia Church, and to the Sisters of Mercy for Mercy Hospital. (CSWS, photographs by E. A. Wilder.)

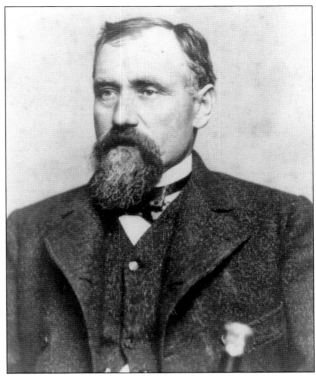

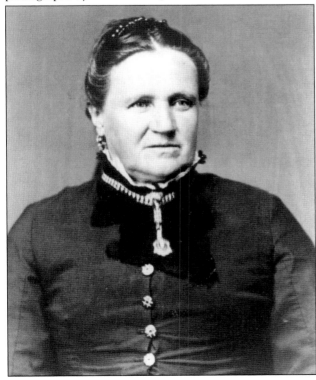

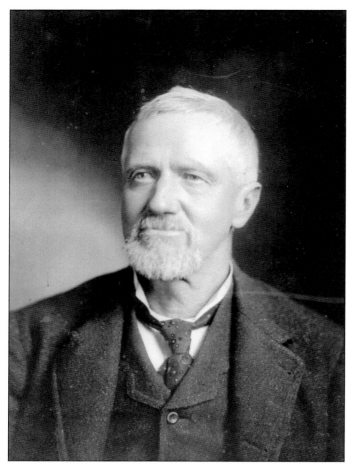

As chronicled by Mary Sloan Ayers in the Daughters of the American Revolution's *Pioneers of the San Juan Country*, Thomas C. Graden (left), one of Durango's most famous entrepreneurs, "arrived in Silverton on July 4, 1876, and in Animas City in 1878, coming over the trail by Molas Lake to the Animas Valley." In 1880, Graden was awarded a tie contract for the Denver and Rio Grande Railroad and became involved in a number of lumber mills in the area, including one at Azotea, New Mexico (below). Ultimately Graden was able to convert his various lumber mills, planing mills, a flour mill, and real estate holdings into the highly successful Graden Mercantile Company in Durango, whose business he directed until 1893. He also served one term as mayor of Durango and was elected to the state legislature. (LPCHS.)

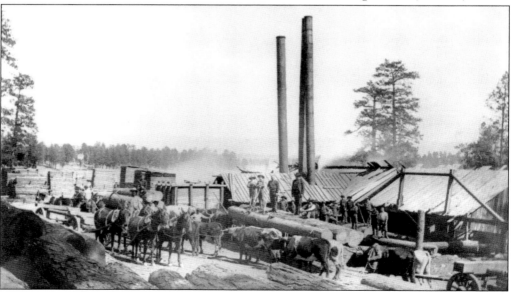

Three

THE D&RG RAILROAD AND DURANGO

The Denver and Rio Grande (D&RG) Railroad Company was organized in Denver by Gen. William Jackson Palmer and ex-governor Alexander Cameron Hunt on October 27, 1870. At first, Palmer and Hunt planned for their railroad to go from Denver to El Paso, Texas, and eventually down into Mexico. One of Palmer's old friends, William A. G. Bell, however, told Palmer about the gold and silver strikes in the San Juans, and it was decided the railroad should head there. The first segment of rails was laid over La Veta Pass in 1876, continuing on to Salida and Alamosa in 1878, and then on to Antonito and up the Cumbres Pass to Chama, New Mexico, in 1880.

After gold and silver mines on the upper Animas began paying off, the D&RG began looking for a way to extend their line to Silverton, Colorado. The logical site for headquartering the Silverton branch, of course, would be the town established on the Animas in 1876, Animas City. Hunt and Bell, however, selected another site downriver for their railroad community, soon to be known as the town of Durango. Consequently, Bell—as chief trustee of the Durango Trust, the company organized to purchase the town site and coal lands in the area—purchased 160 acres for the proposed town site of Durango on April 14, 1880.

In October 1880, realizing Silverton wasn't the best location for a smelter, John A. Porter, executive director of the San Juan Smeltering and Mining Company, moved his smelter from Silverton to the new town of Durango.

Meanwhile, under the able management of Bell, the Durango Trust became converted to the Durango Land and Coal Company. Among their many acquisitions were the coal mines run by Porter.

On August 5, 1881, the D&RG arrived in Durango and promptly began building its line along the Animas River to Silverton, arriving there the following year.

Ten years later, the entrepreneur Otto Mears built the Rio Grande Southern line, running from Durango to Ridgway, Colorado, in order to service the mines in Rico, Ophir, and Telluride, as well as to provide another route to Denver via Montrose and Gunnison. The Rio Grande Southern also tapped the local coal mines at Porter and Perin's Peak, which kept the trains running.

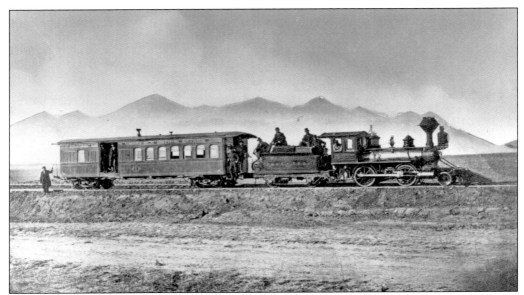

The Denver and Rio Grande Railroad finished laying the first section of track from Denver to Colorado Springs in October 1871 (above). The train didn't arrive in Durango, however, until August 1881. Because the railroad wound tortuously through the mountains on the way, the rails were narrow gauge (3 feet wide) rather than standard (4 feet, 8.5 inches wide).

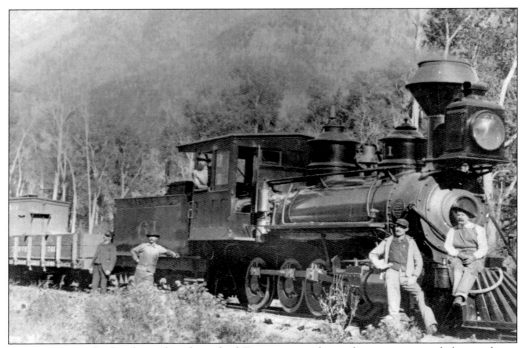

As soon as tracks for the railroad reached Durango, work was begun to extend the tracks to Silverton. Laying tracks up the Animas Valley was relatively easy. Upon reaching Rockwood, however, it became much more difficult. (LPCHS.)

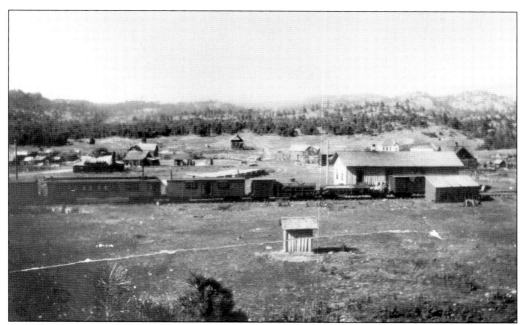

Rockwood (above) was the terminus of the D&RG for a short while, until a bed for the railroad continuing north was gouged out of the canyon walls lining the rugged Animas Gorge. (Mary Ann Lechner.)

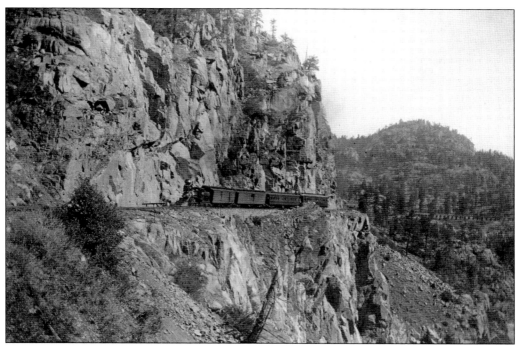

Laying tracks on the "high line" through the Animas Gorge (above) was largely completed in February 1882, reportedly at a cost of $1,000 a foot. (LPCHS.)

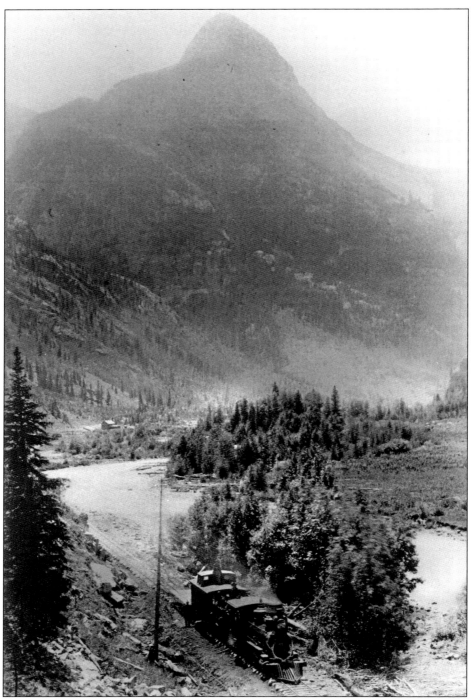

Continuing north, building their last bridge across Mineral Creek in June, the D&RG finally arrived in Silverton in July 1882. In 1887 and 1895, spur lines built by Otto Mears extended to mines outlying from the area, increasing silver production in the county over and above the million-dollar mark it had achieved in 1885. (LPCHS; photograph by W. H. Jackson.)

Palmer (right), organizer and brigadier general of the 15th Pennsylvania Cavalry during the Civil War, gained his experience with railroading first with the Pennsylvania Railroad and then with the Kansas Pacific. Taking charge of the Kansas Pacific Railroad survey, he came west in 1867–1868 and thereafter began developing communities in Colorado, including Colorado Springs and Durango. It is believed that Durango, Colorado, was named after Durango, Mexico, by Gov. Alexander Hunt (below, far left, at Colorado Springs around 1871). According to Helen M. Searcy in the DAR's *Pioneers of the San Juan Country*, "The first house on the mesa, located on 8th Street, between 2nd and 3rd Avenues" was built by land agent James Luttrell for Governor Hunt to stay in when he came to Durango in the spring of 1880. (DPL.)

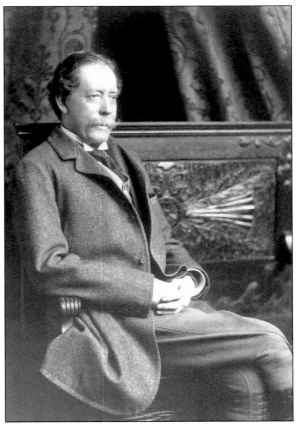

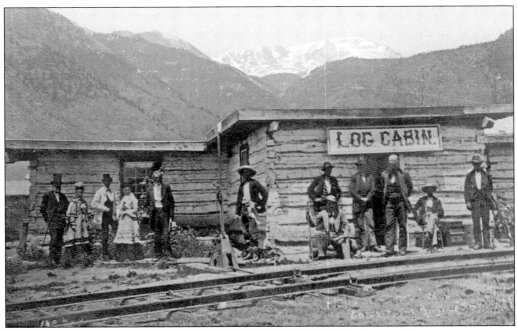

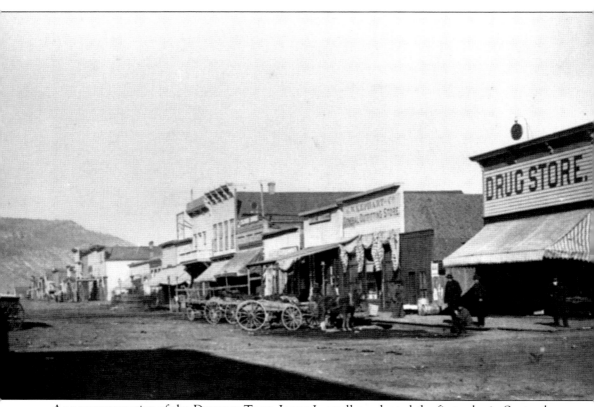

As a representative of the Durango Trust, James Luttrell conducted the first sales in September 1880—immediately after the town site was surveyed by Charles Perin—selling 80 lots the first day. Again, according to Searcy, it was also Luttrell who squired A. P. Camp around the town site and informed him of the plans to make Main Avenue (above, in the 1880s) "the wholesale street," Second Avenue "for retail business," and Third Avenue "a street one hundred and twenty-five feet wide . . . the Boulevard . . . to have rows of trees down the middle like Colorado Springs." Camp was so impressed he moved his bank in Animas City to Durango the following March. (LPCHS.)

In October 1880, John A. Porter (at right) moved the San Juan Smelter (below) from Silverton to Durango. Porter, the "thirty-year-old Connecticut-born metallurgist and smelterman had ridden into the San Juans in the mid-1870's, then gone to Eureka, Nevada, before being lured back to Silverton as manager of the smelter," writes Duane A. Smith in *Rocky Mountain Boom Town.* "Realizing that Silverton did not provide the best locale for a smelter," Smith continues, "he recommended the move. Undoubtedly, he was influenced by the railroad's plans; perhaps the two cooperated because the smelter would provide a tremendous market for the Rio Grande." At any rate, "Durango acquired a significant industry, one that grew into a regional smelting center under Porter's skilled guidance," notes Smith. (LPCHS.)

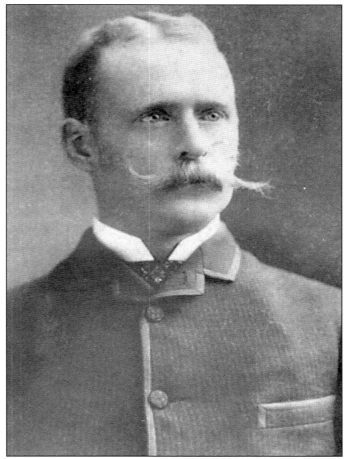

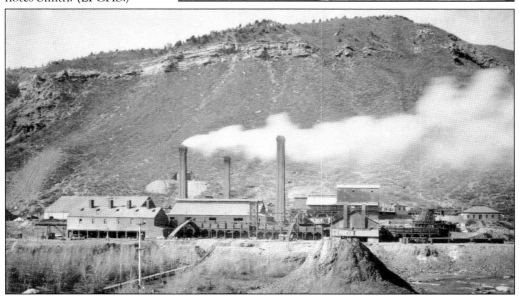

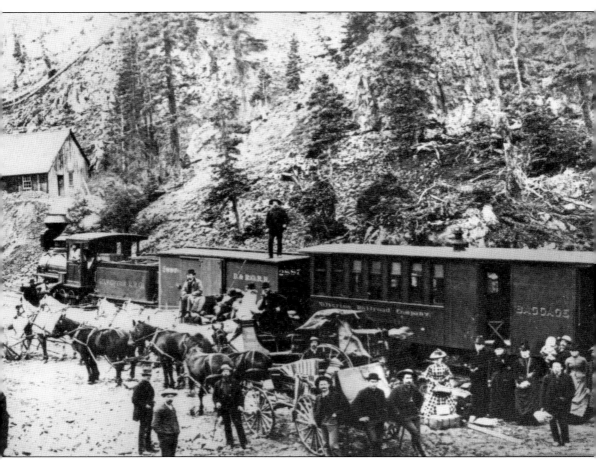

The Denver and Rio Grande not only transported ore, supplies, and passengers between Silverton and Durango, but it also opened up an agricultural market in the Animas Valley. As a result, Smith notes in *Rocky Mountain Boom Town*, the railroad "caused farm property of the Animas Valley [in 1882] to double in appraised valuation over twelve months, with good land selling for as high as $100 per acre." (LPCHS.)

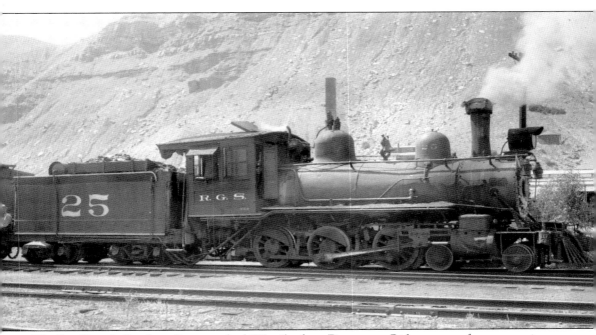

The Rio Grande Southern line stretched 172 miles from Durango to Ridgway, over four mountain passes and 142 bridges, providing access to agricultural markets all over western Colorado. The Southern also boosted tourism in the area, completing the "Circle Route" from Denver to Durango to Ouray and then back to Denver again. (LPCHS.)

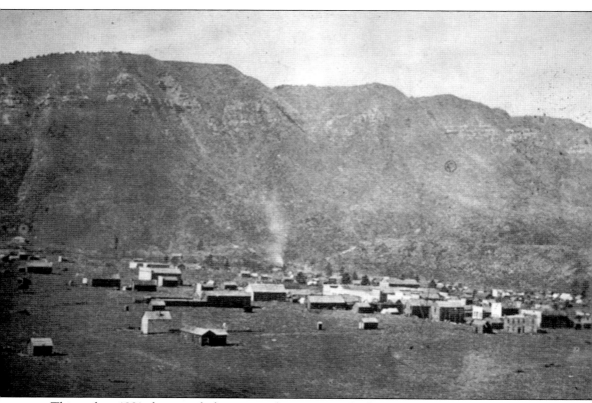

This early c. 1881 photograph documents the extent to which Durango was growing shortly after its inception. By mid-November 1880, according to Smith in *Rocky Mountain Boom Town*, Durango "had seven hotels and restaurants, two blacksmith shops, two bakeries, eleven saloons, dance halls, meat markets, general stores, and a variety of other businesses." Moreover, the population of Durango was approaching 2,000. (LPCHS.)

Four

EARLY ENTREPRENEURS

Immediately after its founding in 1880, the new town of Durango began taking hold.

The oldest businesses in the city, the railroad and the smelter, were thriving. By 1882, the Denver and Rio Grande was promoting its train up the Animas Canyon to Silverton, and John C. Porter's smelter was ready for smelting ores from nearby mines. By 1887, the San Juan and New York Mining and Smelting Company had smelted over $1 million worth of gold, silver, lead, and copper, making it the ninth most productive smelter in Colorado.

Most of the coal for the train and the smelter came from the Durango Coal Mine, established in 1881, and the Porter Coal Mine, established in 1890.

The Durango Trust was also doing well. By 1884, a total of 840 of the original 1,780 lots in Durango had been sold. By 1892, the trust—by then known as the Durango Land and Coal Company—had developed several subdivisions in town. The company also organized the Durango Railway and Realty Company, which operated a trolley in town, horse-drawn in 1891 and converted to electricity in 1893.

Meanwhile, the Durango Trust had donated land on Second Avenue for the county seat and land on Third Avenue for churches and a school. Also the "Boulevard" (as Third Avenue was known then) was becoming the site of luxury homes, Ernest Amy's mansion among the finest.

Elsewhere in town, business was booming. Caroline Westcott Romney brought the first newspaper, the *Durango Record*, to town in 1880. Alfred P. Camp moved the Bank of the San Juan from Animas City to town in 1881. Harry Jackson opened a carriage works and hardware store, Charles Newman a drugstore, Isaak Krushke a dry goods store, and Henry Strater a hotel.

Then disaster struck. In 1889, seven blocks went up in flames, resulting in over half a million dollars' worth of damages. But worse, in 1893, the repeal of the Sherman Silver Purchase Act brought on an economic depression in Durango that lasted until the end of the century. With the collapse of the price of silver, local businesses failed, nearby mines closed, the smelter closed and eventually sold, and the Rio Grande Southern Railroad went into receivership.

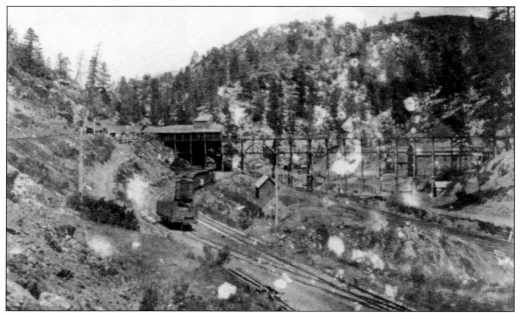

After Durango was founded, a number of coal mines sprung up in the area, including the Porter (above), Hesperus, and Perin's Peak mines west of town, the City (below) to the southwest, and the Black Diamond, Champion, Peerless, and San Juan mines south and east. Closer to town were the Durango Coal Mine and the mine at Reservoir Hill. The local bituminous coal, it turned out, was excellent for coking, a process for heating the coal in ovens to reduce impurities, resulting in coke that could be fired at high temperatures for smelting ores and blacksmithing. Twelve coking ovens were located on Lightner Creek, just west of town. In 1883, local coal mines were producing 12,000 tons per year. By 1890, production had grown to 33,000 tons, ranking the district 10th in the state. (LPCHS.)

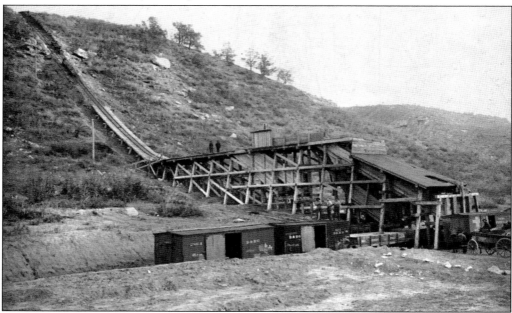

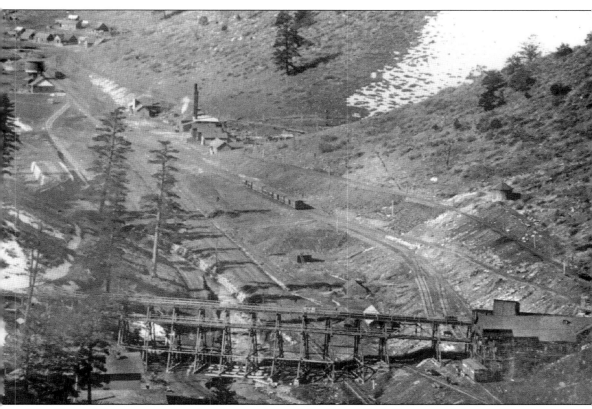

The Porter Mine—opened under the auspices of the Porter Fuel Company, John A. Porter, president, and William A. G. Bell, vice president—was the largest coal mine in the Durango area. In 1892, the mine boasted 80 percent of the district's production. In 1899, the Porter and the Hesperus, both owned by the same company, produced over 80,000 tons of coal, employing 108 miners. The population of the town of Porter (above), located next to the mine on the Rio Grande Southern, eventually grew to 144 and included a general store. However, the repeal of the Sherman Silver Purchase Act in 1893, the economic depression that accompanied it, and the smelter strike of 1899 forced the closing of many of the coal mines in the area, including the Porter. In 1906, the Porter was sold to the Union Pacific Coal Company. In 1908, the mine and the town around it were abandoned. (Archie Bodo.)

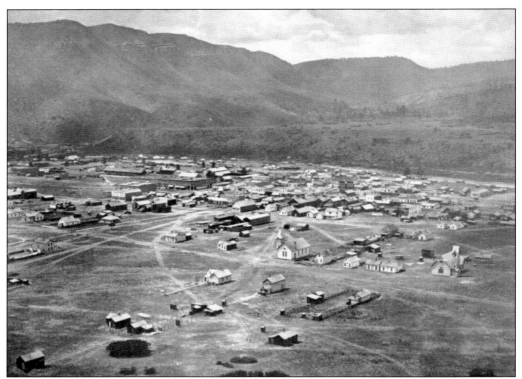

By December 1880, the *Daily Record* reports, 134 businesses had located in Durango (shown here around 1885), including 12 lawyers, 3 physicians, 2 dressmakers, a tailor, a church, and 3 newspapers. The *Daily Record* was one of those newspapers—the first, in fact—brought here by Caroline Westcott Romney from Leadville in 1880 and operating from a tent on Second Avenue. (LPCHS.)

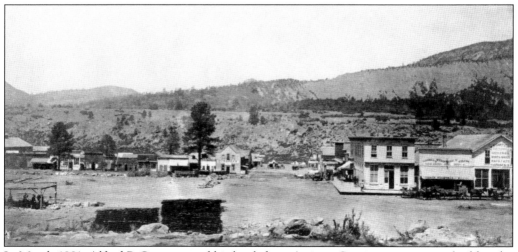

In March 1881, Alfred P. Camp moved his bank from Animas City into a two-story building he and John L. McNeil constructed on Main Avenue and Ninth Street in Durango, later to become the First National Bank (right of center). To the left of the bank, on Railroad Street, can be seen the "Hanging Tree," where Henry Read Moorman was lynched on April 16, 1881. (LPCHS.)

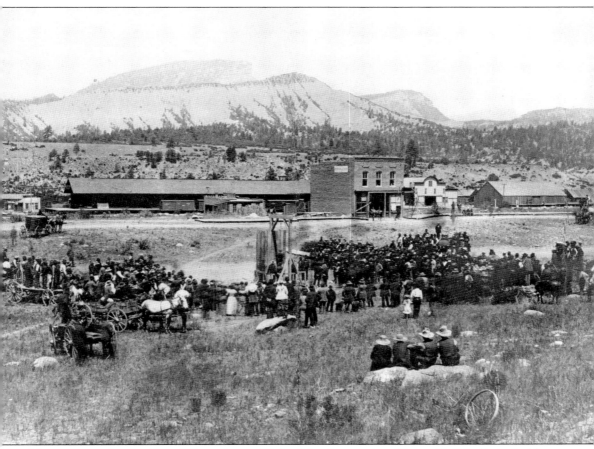

Moorman was lynched by a "Committee of Safety" for the murder of James K. Prindle in "cold blood," reported the *Daily Record*, at a "notorious amusement place" known as the Coliseum. The following day—after being served notice by another Committee of Safety to get out of town—the infamous Stockton and Eskridge gang was able to escape Moorman's fate, though Ike Stockton was later shot down in Durango by county sheriff Jim Sullivan and bled to death. Stockton lies buried in the Animas City Cemetery. The only legal hanging in Durango took place on June 23, 1882, across the street from where the Strater now stands. On that date, George N. Woods was hanged for the murder of M. C. Buchanan at the Pacific Club Saloon. (CSWS; photograph by Gonner and Leeka.)

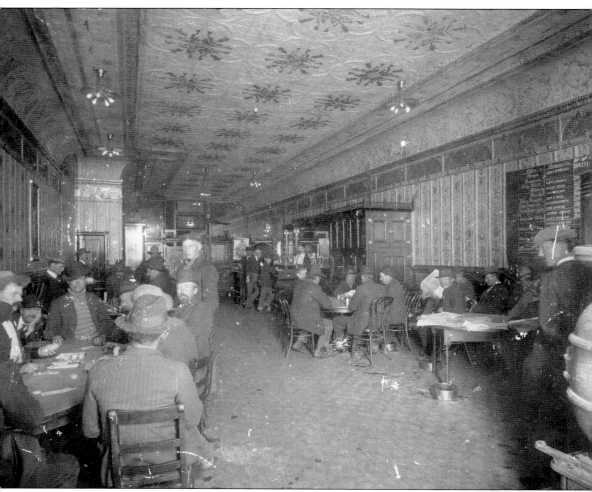

Most of the saloons were located in the 900 block of Main Avenue and the "red-light district," between the railroad and the river. El Moro Saloon is shown here around 1899. The most famous "madam" in the district was Bessie Rivers, "a shrewd businesswoman who made regular deposits in A. P. Camp's First National Bank," writes Duane A. Smith in *Durango Diary*. Bessie's businesses continued well into the 1900s, ultimately being taken over by Betty Hacker. Longtime resident Archie Bodo used to tell a story about Neil Camp, president of the First National after his father, A. P., died. "I was serviceman for Norge appliances," starts Archie, "and one Sunday I got a call from Betty. We just put in a refrigerator for her and she says, 'There's a noise in it and it's just running me crazy. . . .' So . . . I stopped right in front of the house, and . . . I wasn't in but just a few minutes and I came out and my wife said, 'I seen Mr. Camp come out of the back door there and go up the street. What's he doin' here?' " (CSWS; photograph by Gonner and Leeka.)

A. P. Camp (right) and
John McNeil came from Del Norte
to Animas City to establish the
Bank of the San Juan in 1880,
changing its name to the Bank
of Durango when it moved to
Durango in 1881. It ultimately
became the First National Bank
of Durango in 1885. Camp started
his banking career as a cashier and
then served as president from 1889
until his death in 1925. (CSWS;
photograph by Brand.)

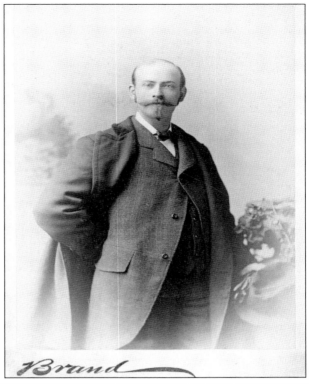

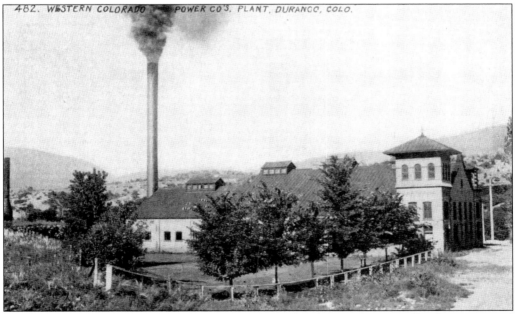

Alternating-current power came to Durango in 1887, thanks to James Luttrell, John Porter, and
T. C. Graden, among others. The Western Colorado Power Company not only provided electric
lighting for Durango—replacing gas lights—but also powered the city's streetcar system, promoted
and superintended by T. C. Graden. (CSWS.)

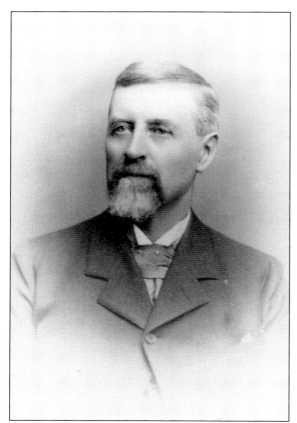

Robert E. Sloan (left) came west with T. C. Graden on a tie contract for the D&RG. Both Sloan and Graden had served under railroad founder General Palmer during the Civil War. In 1894, Sloan and his wife, the former Hannah T. Sullenberger, moved from Denver to Durango to partner in Graden's mercantile business, which at the time included the recently purchased Guyles-Graden Flour Mill (below). In 1914, Graden retired and moved to Hollywood, California, where he died in 1924. From that time on, Sloan assumed operation of the mercantile company until his death in 1932. Thereafter, the company was run by Sloan's son Robert H. Sloan, who had joined the firm in 1893. (LPCHS.)

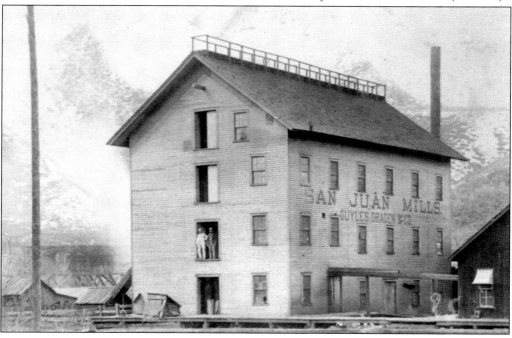

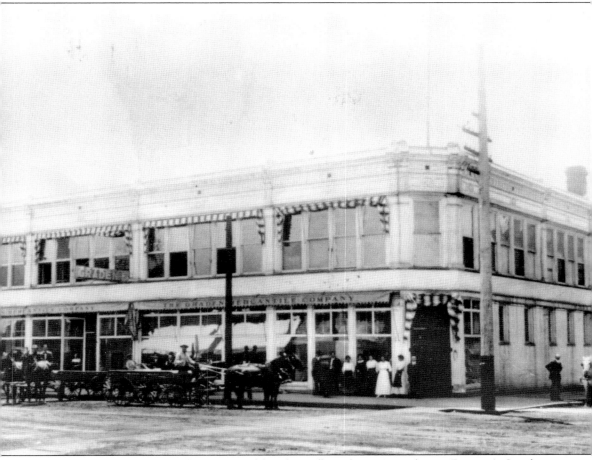

By 1894, the Graden Mercantile Company (above) was flourishing. According to Duane A. Smith in *Durango Diary*, prices at the mercantile store in 1894 were listed as follows: flour, $1.75 per 100 pounds; sugar, $1 for 16 pounds; tomatoes, $1 for seven cans; soda or oyster crackers, 10¢ per pound; fresh ranch eggs, 20¢ per dozen; rice, $1 for 15 pounds; matches, 25¢ for 17 boxes; baking powder, 35¢ for 1-pound can; ginger snaps, 15¢ per pound; coffee, 20¢ per pound; and soap, $1 for 22 bars. "The best California wines," adds Smith, "cost 50 cents per bottle, while the 'best' whiskeys ranged from $2.50 to $7 a bottle." (LPCHS.)

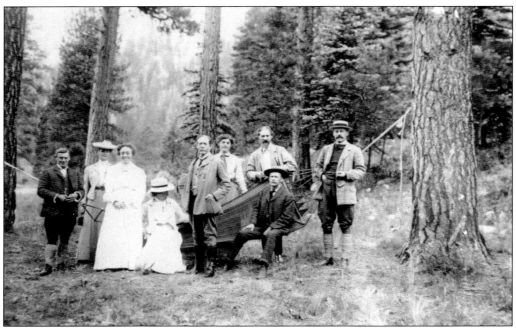

In 1891, John Porter (above, seated at right) and General Palmer (standing at center)—as vice president and president of the Durango Land and Coal Company respectively—invested in Durango's first streetcar under the auspices of the Durango Railway and Realty Company. In 1892, as reported by Duane A. Smith in *Rocky Mountain Boom Town*, the "experiment with a horse-drawn streetcar line down Main Avenue" changed over to electric power (below). As a result, continues Smith, "Overcoming ice . . . and breakdowns, the two cars clanged up and down Main from the depot to Animas City, passing each other on double tracks just beyond the river bridge, a bargain ride for a nickel fare." One year later, however, "their one-fifth interest in the Durango Railway and Realty Company . . . had not made a dime in profits." (LPCHS.)

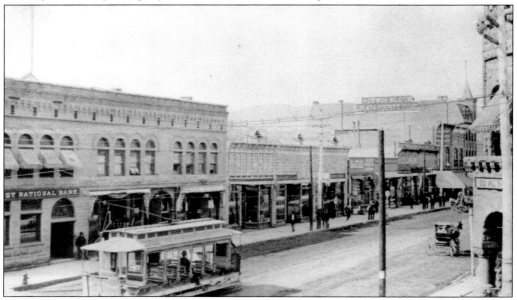

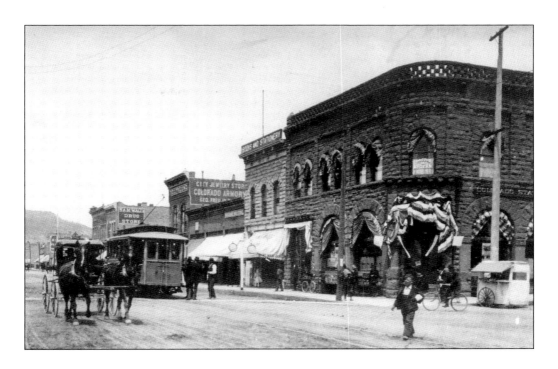

In 1887, the Colorado State Bank (above, at right) became one of the leaders in Durango's financial community. In 1907, however, as a result of a nationwide economic panic, the Colorado State Bank failed and the Burns National Bank (bottom, at left) took over. Built in 1892, the Colorado State Bank building at Ninth Street and Main Avenue, now known as the Burns Bank building, is one of the few prominent Richardsonian Romanesque–style buildings in Durango. The familiar fortress-like design is typical to areas that were experiencing commercial prosperity around the turn of the 20th century. (LPCHS.)

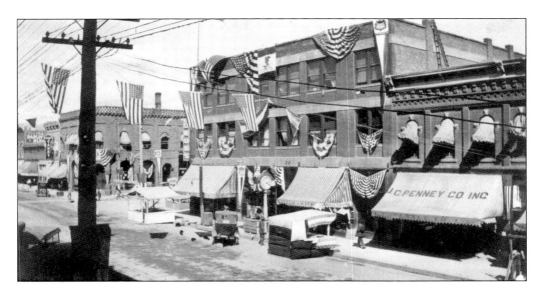

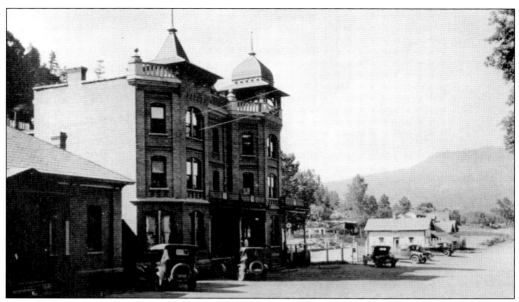

The Burns National Bank owes its beginnings to Thomas Daniel Burns, a merchant and landowner from Rio Arriba County, New Mexico. Burns was a shrewd businessman. In New Mexico, he was able to expand his holdings by purchasing a good part of the Martinez land grant from small landowners through default. Just before the 20th century began, Burns decided to extend his land holdings, buying acreage in Ignacio and the Animas Valley. In 1892, Burns purchased the Trimble Hot Springs resort, including the "splendid brick hotel" (shown here in the 1920s), where he and his family spent most of their summers. As reported by Smith in *Durango Diary*, "Trimble Springs, nine miles north of the city limits, advertised 'curative qualities unsurpassed,' and a fine bar and billiards room." (LPCHS.)

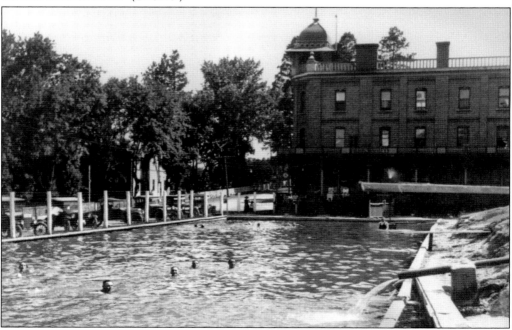

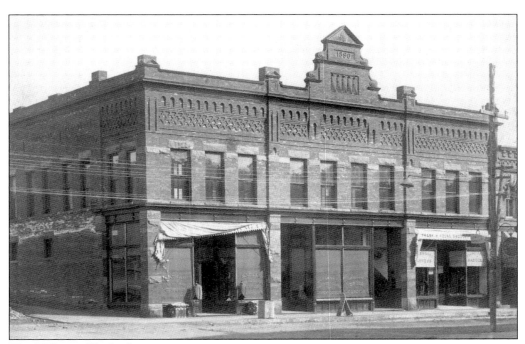

The Williams Block, the south end of the 900 block of Main Avenue, housed Nathan's clothing store, Parson's Drug store, Young's saddle shop, and Hahn's jewelry store. Parson's Drug, which was also located here before this building was built, was where Bruce Hunt, son of Gov. A. C. Hunt, bled to death after being shot by a bank robber making his escape from the Bank of Durango. Parson's later moved across the street (see page 59, bottom photograph). Charles M. Williams (at right), vice president of the Bank of Durango at the time of the robbery, also owned two lots across the street in the 700 block of Main that he later sold to Harry Jackson for his carriage shop. (Above, DPL; photograph by Gonner and Leeka; right, CSWS; photograph by Charles E. Emery.)

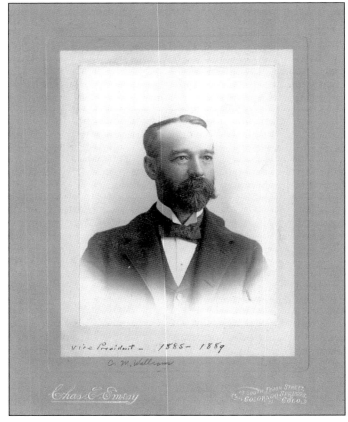

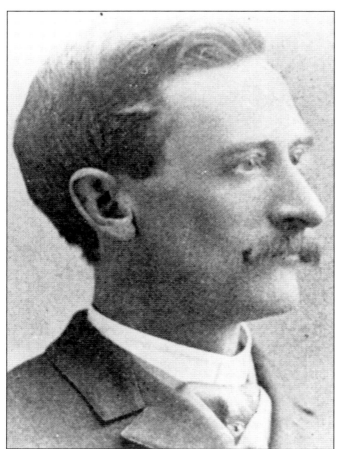

In 1879, Charles Newman (left) came with his partners Thomas Chestnut and William L. Stephens from Del Norte to Silverton, started a drugstore there, and then moved to Animas City and started a drugstore there. In 1881, Newman and his wife, Marian—sister of Chestnut—moved to Durango and started a drugstore here. "At one time," according to Edna Newman Sheets in *Pioneers of the San Juan Country*, "the firm of Newman, Chestnut & Stephens operated a chain of six drug stores." Newman made his money in mines, however, and eventually sold all his drugstores, the one in Durango to Sam Wall. In 1893, Newman built the three-story, red sandstone building on Main Avenue that bears his name (below). From 1892 to 1896, Newman represented Colorado's 19th District as state senator. (Left, LPCHS; below, CSWS.)

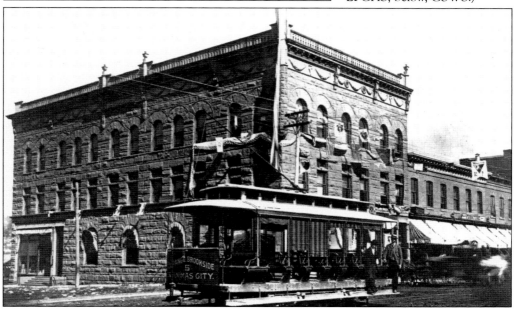

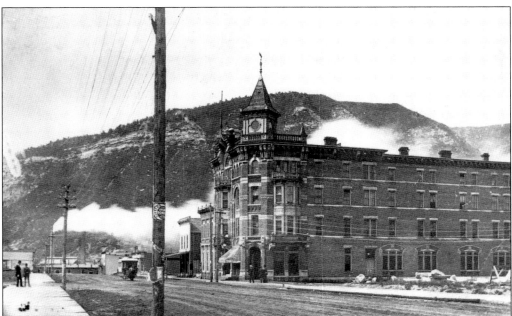

The Strater Hotel (above) and the Grand Central Hotel were considered two of the finest hotels in town. The Grand Central was built by Thomas Rockwood (at right, holding son Gilbert around 1910) in 1880. The Strater, built by Henry Stater in 1888 and added onto in 1892, "earned the most praise," writes Smith in *Durango Diary*, "but it was challenged by eight competitors, 'all good hotels.'" Those competing hotels included not only the Grand Central but also the Columbian and National hotels, as well as the Peeples Hotel, later to become the Rochester Hotel, on Second Avenue. In 1893, Smith notes, "Rooms . . . could be secured at the Strater and Columbian hotels for $3 to $4, and at the National for $2.50." (Above, CSWS; right, LPCHS; photograph by Pennington and Updike.)

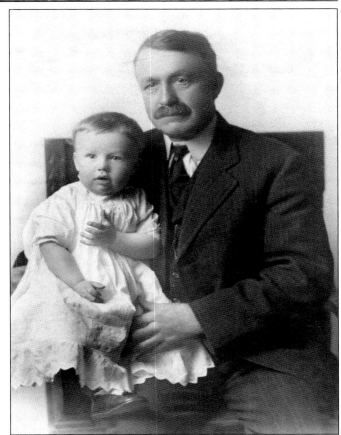

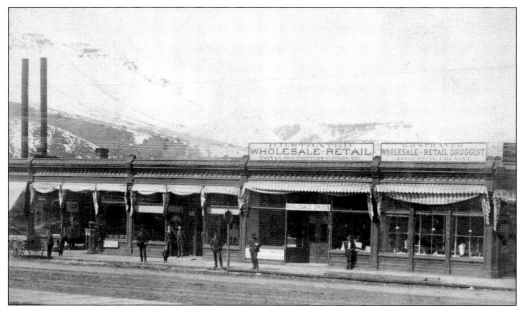

In 1892, the north end of the west side of the 700 block of Main Avenue was known as the Union Block. H. H Strater's Wholesale and Retail Paints store was located there, as well as T. C. Graden's Brooms, later to become part of the Graden Mercantile building. (DPL; photograph by Gonner and Leeka.)

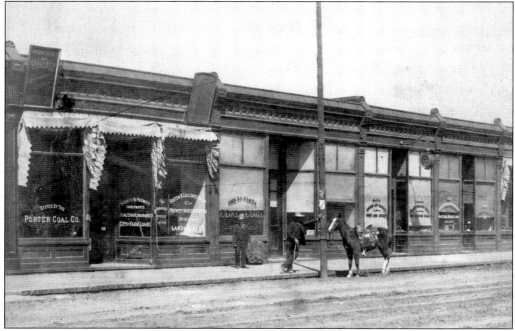

In 1892, the south end of the west side of the 700 block of Main Avenue—continuing the row of commercial buildings with ornate dentils, bracketed cornices, and pilasters on that block—housed the Porter Coal Company, Prewitt and Prewitt Investments, the La Plata Coal and Coke Company, and Bijou Wines and Liquors. (DPL; photograph by Gonner and Leeka.)

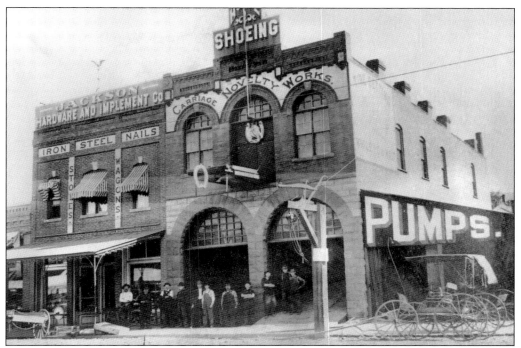

Harry Jackson arrived in Durango in 1881, boarding at the National Hotel. In 1883, he married Louisa Becker, daughter of the proprietor of the hotel. In 1884, Jackson passed on an opportunity to buy two lots on Main Avenue from C. M. Williams for $1,000 and ended up paying $4,500 for them three years later. Jackson's carriage and blacksmith business flourished until 1893, when he turned to selling hardware. (LPCHS.)

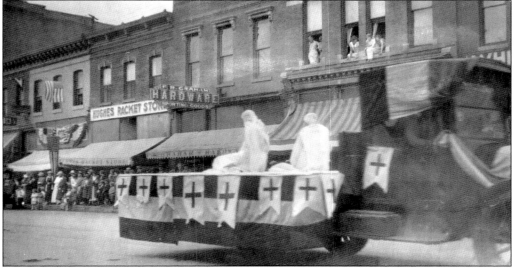

Among other hardware stores in Durango was one of the Alva Adams chain, which had been in town since the 1880s. In 1894, Fergus R. Graham—the accountant and one of the major stockholders of the store—purchased the business. Graham's Hardware (above) remained on the 800 block of Main Avenue for more than 60 years. (LPCHS.)

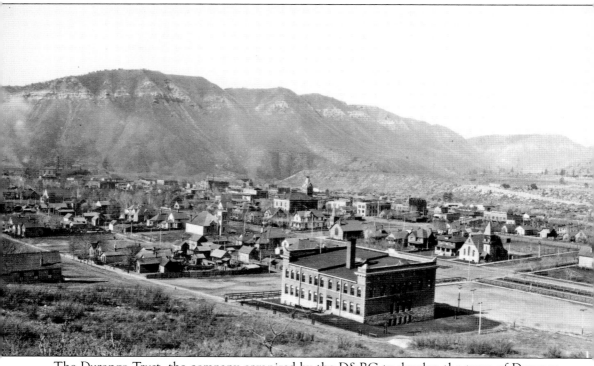

The Durango Trust, the company organized by the D&RG to develop the town of Durango, set aside land for public buildings and churches. In 1881, Durango wrested the county seat from Parrot and in 1891 built the county courthouse on land reserved for it on Second Avenue (the building with clock tower in center). In 1893, the high school was built on land reserved for it on Third Avenue (foreground). The top floor of the building housed the high school and the lower floors the lower grades. The first high school classes in Durango were held in Longfellow School, the public school on East Second Avenue, graduating its first class of 33 students in 1889. (DPL; photograph by George L. Beam.)

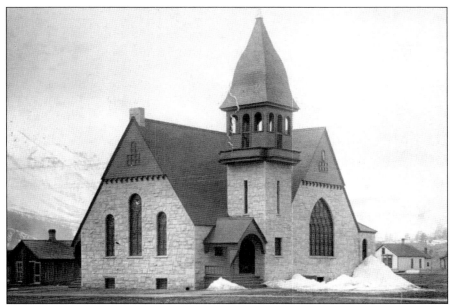

The Presbyterian and Methodist churches on Third Avenue, as well as the original wooden St. Mark's Church on Second Avenue, were destroyed in the fire of July 1, 1889. St. Mark's was rebuilt in brick on Third in 1892. The Presbyterians (above) and Methodists (below) rebuilt soon after. The First Baptist Church survived the fire, but the Baptists built a larger church on Third in 1901. The Southern Methodists had built their "Little Stone Church" across the river in north Durango in 1882. The Catholics had built St. Columba's Church also across the river—on land donated by Peter Fassbinder—in 1881. (LPCHS.)

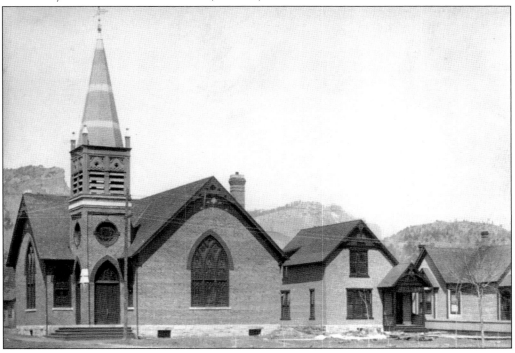

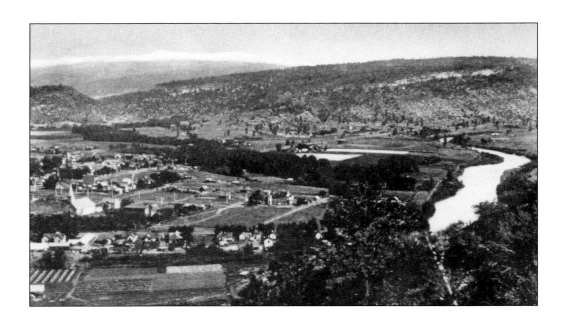

The Catholic complex surrounding St. Columba's Church (above, left) included St. Mary's Academy and the Sisters of Mercy Hospital (above, center, and below), the only general hospital in the Southwest. In 1893, St. Mary's Academy, on the site where the St. Columba School is now, numbered some 100 students. The Sisters of Mercy, who first operated St. Mary's Academy as a convent, came to Durango in 1882 expressly to care for the sick in the mining camps of southwestern Colorado. In 1884, a two-story building of native white sandstone was built to house Mercy Hospital for this purpose (below). The source of water for the hospital came from a spring on the Fassbinder homestead (above, foreground), the same spring he tapped to provide water for the town of Durango. (LPCHS.)

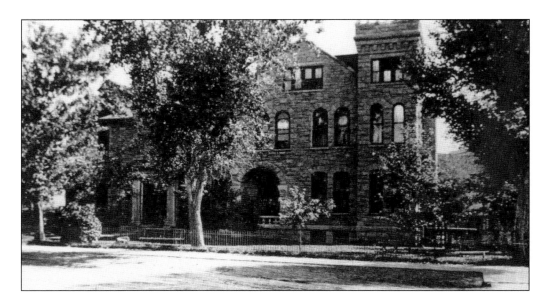

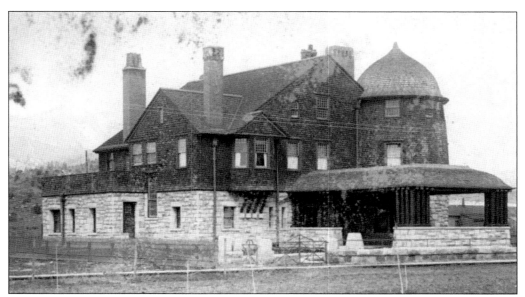

Ernest J. H. Amy, superintendent of the smelter and son of the president of the San Juan and New York Mining and Smelting Company, built the most elegant residence on Third Avenue (above), now the Hood Mortuary, supposedly in order to lure his wife here from back east. Built in 1888 at a cost of nearly $50,000, the inside of Amy's house was finished in natural wood panels, reportedly provided by Pullman. Alfred P. Camp, president of the First National Bank, also built his house on Third (below). (Above, LPCHS; below, CSWS.)

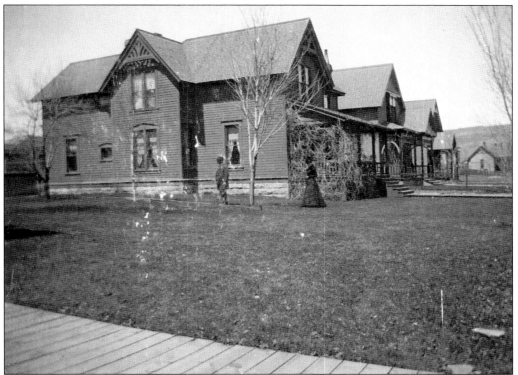

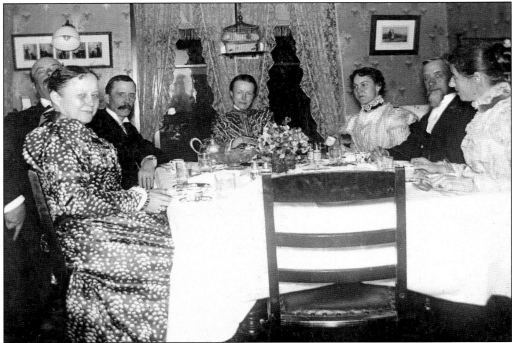

A. P. Camp (above, second from left) and his wife, Estelle (center)—sister of Camp's partner at the bank, John McNeil—were the center of social life in Durango. A. P. was one of the first presidents of the Board of Trade, city treasurer in 1884, and an early member of the school board. Estelle was a member of the Colorado Cliff Dwellings Association, the Reading Club, the Ladies Library Club, and the Daughters of the American Revolution. Adjacent to the Camp house on Third Avenue is a sister Queen Anne–style house (below, right), built in 1892 by William P. Vaile (above, sixth from left), who ultimately became treasurer at the First National Bank. (Above, LPCHS; below, CSWS.)

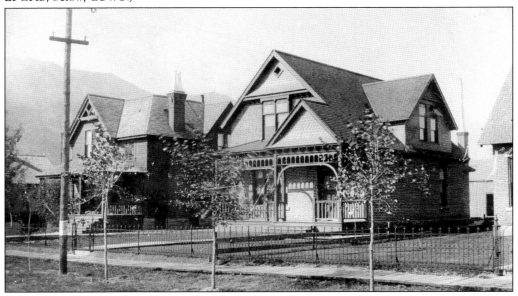

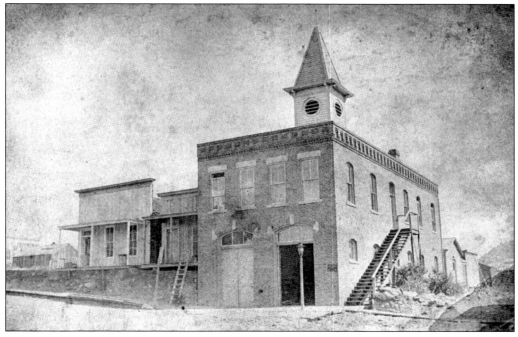

Durango after the big fire

All the efforts of the local fire department couldn't prevent the half-million dollars worth of damages to property wreaked by the fire of July 1, 1889 (above, looking up Tenth Street, center). With a strong wind from the west behind it, the fire spread from downtown Durango to Third Avenue. Among the buildings destroyed were 11 stores, 6 saloons, 4 restaurants, 3 churches, and 35 homes. Also gone was the county courthouse on Second Avenue, as well as city hall and the fire house itself on Tenth Street, between Main and Second Avenues (below). As noted by Smith in *Durango Diary,* "Less half the loss was covered by insurance. . . . A mass meeting, held in the afternoon," however, "raised twelve hundred dollars within an hour to help the poor and destitute." (LPCHS; photographs by Gonner and Leeka.)

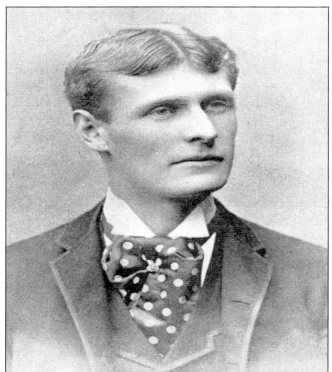

In 1888, Porter sold the San Juan and New York Mining and Smelting Company to New York banker Henry Amy, to be managed by his son Ernest Amy (left). After the crash of 1893, however, silver dropped from $1.35 per ounce to less than 50¢. Consequently, in 1894, Ernest Amy was forced to close the smelter, sell his Third Avenue home, and return east. (Duane A. Smith.)

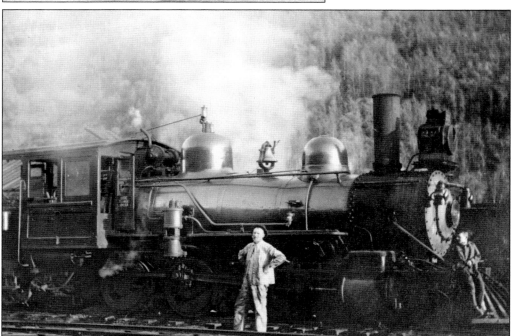

With the price of silver plummeting and the resulting depression, railroad business was cut in half. Then in 1894, the railroad unions struck against the Pullman Company, the D&RG temporarily halted its run to Durango, and the Rio Grande Southern went bankrupt. (LPCHS.)

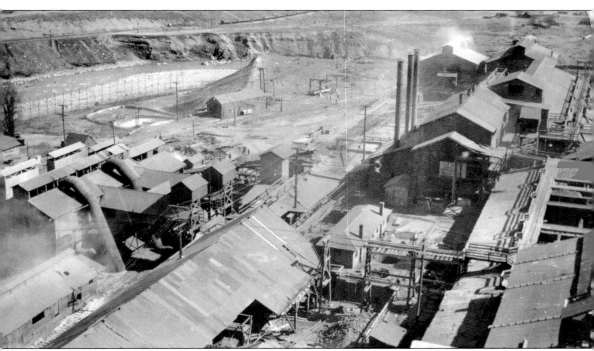

Hit hard by the repeal of the Sherman Silver Purchase Act of 1893, Amy's smelter was eventually sold to Denver's Omaha and Grant Smelting Company and then to the American Smelting and Refining Company, part of the Guggenheim family conglomerate. Surviving labor strikes in 1899 and 1902, however, the ASARCO smelter (above) became one of the most important smelters in Colorado. Employing some 350 locals, by the dawn of the 20th century, the smelter had become the town's chief employer, earning Durango the appropriate title "Smelter City." (LPCHS.)

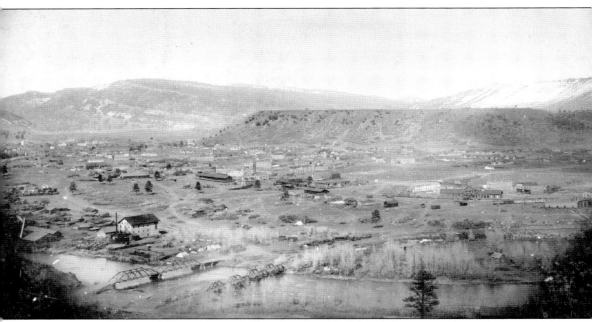

Despite all the hardships Durango suffered at the end of the 19th century, the town continued to prosper and grow. Note the increase of growth apparent in this 1890s panoramic view of Durango. As chronicled by Smith in *Rocky Mountain Boom Town*, Durango's Board of Trade, founded in 1883, was reorganized in 1892 "to advertise the city and promote its interests by disseminating information related to commercial, financial, and industrial affairs." As a measure of its success, Smith continues, annual sales that year amounted to more than $3 million. By 1890, Durango's population—which numbered an estimated 2,500 people in 1880—had grown to nearly 3,400, making it the largest city on the Western Slope. (LPCHS.)

Five

THE WARS AND BETWEEN THE WARS

Considering the economic depression brought about by the repeal of the Sherman Silver Purchase Act in the previous century, the temporary shutting down of the smelter, the general mining strike in the state, and prohibitions against gambling and drinking, not to mention a flood and a flu epidemic, the excitement generated by the advent of World War I was quite positive. Certainly Durango was bursting with patriotism. Moreover, increases in local coal production and tourism contributed to the town's economic recovery.

Coal mining in the area reached an all-time record high, employing 311 miners in 1908. The Porter Mine was the largest. The Hesperus Mine, owned by the same company, and the Calumet Mine at Perin's Peak followed. By 1917 and the beginning of World War I, local coal mines were producing around 140,000 tons per year.

Also a variety of new businesses in town provided a foil to the stock market crash of 1929. John C. Turner, for instance, had founded the Turner Investment Company in 1906. T. D. Burns had opened the Burns Bank in 1910. Frederick W. Kroeger purchased the G. H. Clark seed and feed store. Lester Gardenswartz opened a sporting goods store.

Thanks to the Durango Board of Trade, joining with the Durango Club in 1914 and eventually becoming the chamber of commerce, Durango was also bringing in tourist dollars. Much of the board's work had to do with building roads. By 1917, roads connected Durango to Silverton, Mancos, and the newly created Mesa Verde National Park, as well as to the San Luis Valley via Wolf Creek Pass. And as roads improved, of course, automobiles became more prevalent. As a result, tourists visiting Durango began to number in the thousands.

With the coming of the Great Depression, however, Durango's good fortunes dwindled. Many of the coal mines closed, and the smelter, the largest employer in town, shut down for good.

Only after Pres. Franklin D. Roosevelt instituted his New Deal in 1933 was Durango able to bounce back. WPA-financed projects, employing hundreds, resulted in improvements to local streets and roads, the building of curbs, sidewalks, and bridges, and the building of Smiley School and the La Plata County Fairgrounds.

Then, after the advent of World War II, the U.S. Vanadium Corporation opened a mill where the old smelter used to be to process uranium ore for use in the making of the atomic bomb.

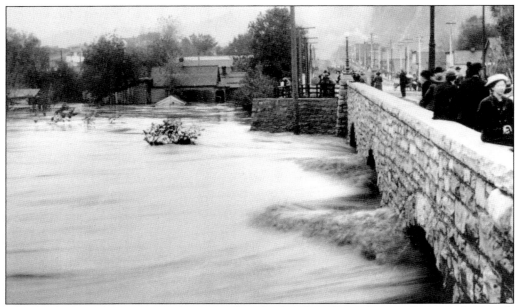

The flood of October 1911 wiped out 22 miles of railroad tracks in Animas Canyon, along with almost 100 bridges. The bridge connecting north and south Durango, however, managed to survive. The flood endangered lives, but not as seriously as the Spanish influenza in 1918. Some 150 people died from the flu in Silverton. Ultimately—as the epidemic raged in Telluride, Rico, and Montrose—Durango quarantined out-of-towners. (LPCHS.)

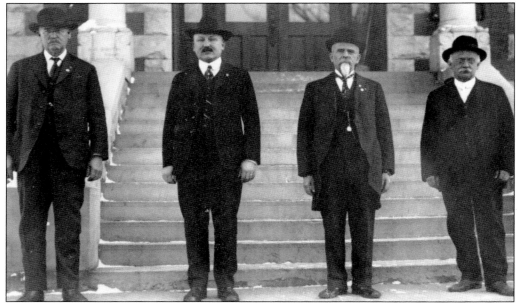

In April 1917, the Durango draft board, including Arthur Fassbinder, son of Peter (left), began interviewing potential draftees for World War I. By the end of the war in November 1918, however, 346 young men from the county ended up enlisting. The Sedgwick Post of the Grand Army of the Republic saw them off at the railroad depot. The Daughters of the American Revolution in Durango organized a "Council of Defense." (CSWS.)

In the first decade of the 20th century, coal mining in La Plata County recovered. City Mine alone produced over 30,000 tons in 1909. Businesses in Durango recovered as well. In 1910, as Duane A. Smith notes in his *Rocky Mountain Boom Town*, "The real heart of Main ran from Seventh through Tenth. . . . A quick survey of the businesses revealed the usual grocery, paint, clothing, hardware, and drug stores, hotels, blacksmiths, real estate offices, restaurants, bakeries, and saloons (twenty-two)." Moreover, "Evidence of the changing times, 'automobile concerns' and moving picture theaters, made their appearance. . . . It was 'solid business community for a town of Durango's size,' " continues Smith, the population totaling "4,686 by the 1910 census." By 1918 (the date of these photographs), Durango was booming again. (Right, LPCHS; photograph by George L. Beam; below, DPL; photograph by Walker Art Studio.)

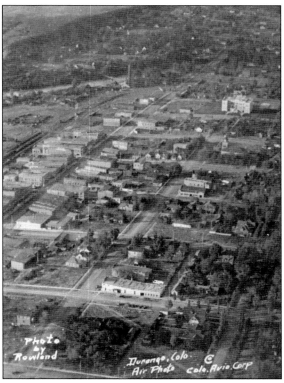

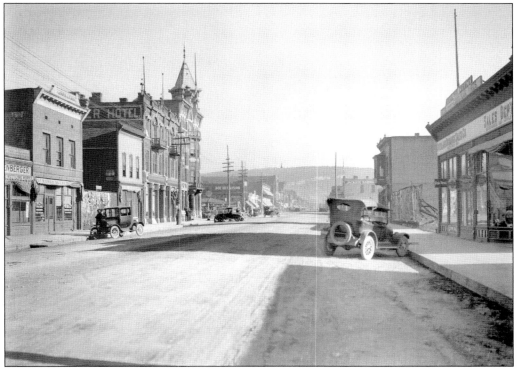

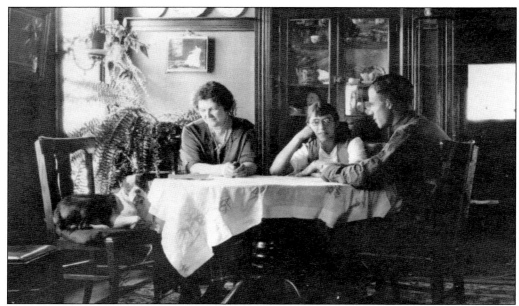

After J. C. Turner died in 1902, his son John William Turner (above, at right) purchased a real estate concern in Durango—becoming the Durango Real Estate Company in 1904 and Turner Investment Company in 1909—located in the old Burns Bank building. Pictured here also in their home at West Second Avenue and Twenty-fifth Street are J. W.'s wife, Josephine (left), and his daughter, Bonnie (center). J. W.'s son, Richard William "Dick" Turner Sr. (below, at left, around 1923), joined his father in the family venture. In this photograph, R. W. and his stenographer Clara Goeglein are seen in their office when it was located in the Strater Hotel building, where the Diamond Belle Saloon is today. In 1955, J. W. Turner established the Turner Industrial Bank, later to become the Bank of Durango, which later yet was sold to Norwest Bank. (Suzie Turner Belt.)

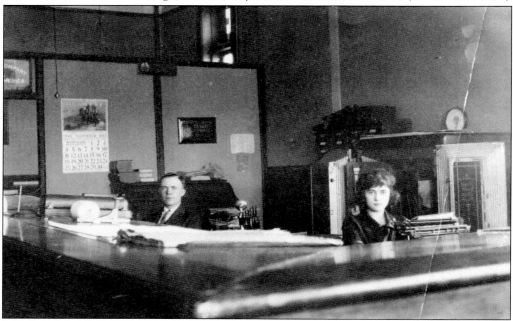

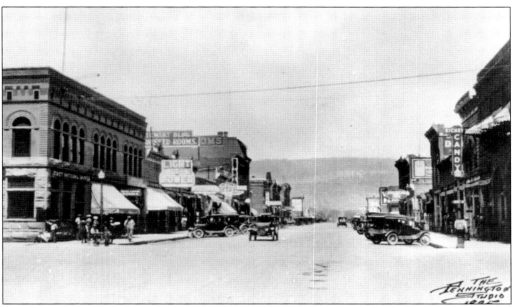

By the 1920s, automobile dealers in town included the Durango Motor Company, the Channel Motor Company, the Pittman Motor Company (above, middle of block), the Butler Garage, and the Webb Motor Company. After opening his business on Main Avenue in 1918, P. W. Pittman (below, second from left) introduced the new "one-ton, worm-drive Fordson" to Durango. In 1925, the Butler Garage was selling the Essex Coach for $995 and three models of Hudsons for $1,983. In 1929, Webb Motors was selling the "Nash 400 special six sedan"—"fully equipped with a spare tire and all the freight handling charges included"—for $1,572. P. W. Pittman later moved his dealership from 945 Main Avenue to 801 East Second Avenue. (Above, DPL; photograph by Pennington Studio; below, Karen Pittman.)

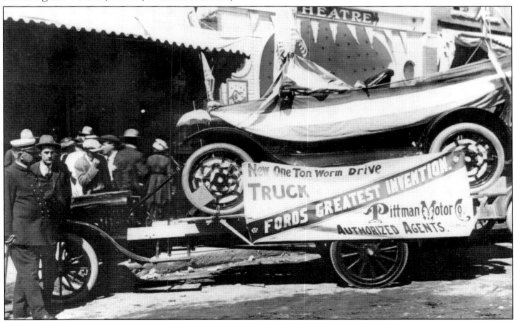

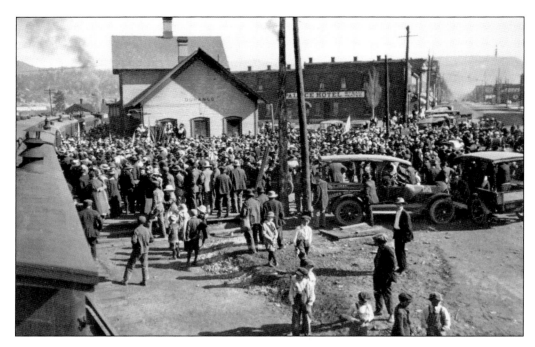

The D&RG depot (above) anchored the businesses on Main Avenue. Up the street from the depot was the Palace Hotel, built in 1895. And farther up the street on the corner was the Hotel Savoy (below, around 1920). "The Savoy's six o'clock Christmas dinner," notes Duane A. Smith in *Durango Diary II*, "featured soups, relishes, meats, fish, roasts, vegetables, salads and desserts, homemade mince and pumpkin pies, old English plum pudding and other treats. All this costs only $1." As Smith also says in *Rocky Mountain Boom Town*, "The south end of Main down near the depot festered. . . . It was a source of trouble with beer parlors, gambling, dance halls, and white slavery. Not until several shootings and a 1939 murder was action finally, but slowly, taken." (Above, LPCHS; below DPL.)

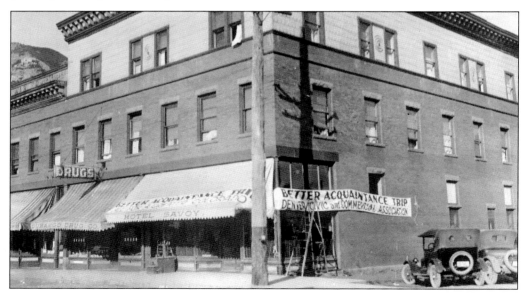

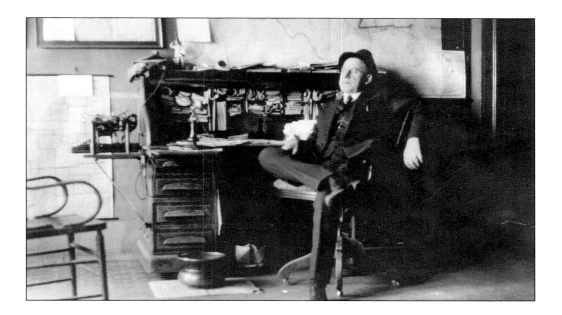

"The most infamous murder between the world wars," continues Smith, "was the one involving the editors of the Democrat and the Herald; it took place on Main in broad daylight, when Rod Day killed William Wood in April 1922. . . . The feud had grown out of newspaper bickering and personal conflicts. Both men were sons of famous San Juan pioneers, and the killing created a scandal. Even though Day eventually was acquitted of murder, he sold his interest in the paper, ending the Durango career of this famous newspaper family." Rod Day (above) took over the *Durango Democrat*, whose offices are pictured below on Main Avenue in 1922, from his father, David Day. Dave Day was known for his acerbic wit, much of it directed at the rival *Herald*. Dave Day wrote for the *Democrat* until his death in 1914. (Suzie Turner Belt.)

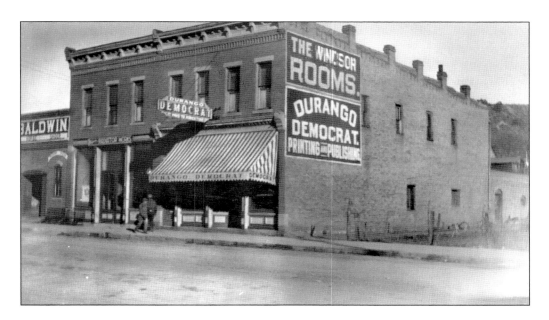

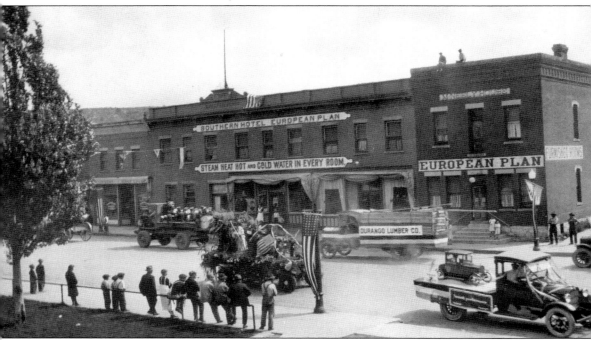

Among some of the more notorious businesses on south Main Avenue, across from the railroad depot, was the Southern Hotel. Longtime resident Nick Zellitti's wife, Mary, describes this section of town: "It was rough." "When I was here in school," says Mary, "I would never walk down there." "Rose Fanto had a bar," adds Nick, "a rowdy place." "And then there was Blue Moon Lil," continues Mary. "She worked out of The Southern Hotel," notes Nick. "And then there was the Linmor Hotel," adds Mary. "Now that was a whore house. . . . But I want to tell you," says Mary, "those were the best people in the world. . . . And they all helped each other," she emphasizes. "If somebody was sick or hurt, everybody helped each other. . . . It was wonderful!" Right next door to the Southern Hotel was the European Grocery Store (above at left), opened in the early 1920s by Nick Zellitti's father, Frank. Frank Zellitti had come to Durango from Italy around 1900. (Suzie Turner Belt.)

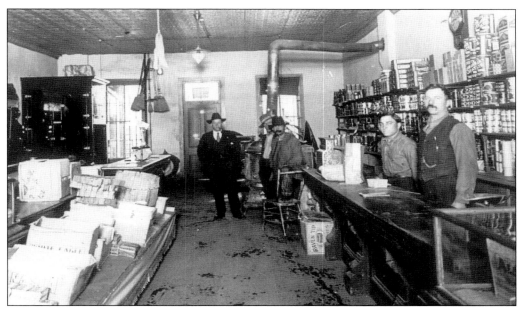

When he was a kid, Nick Zellitti delivered groceries for his father, Frank (above, at right). "For free," says Nick's wife, Mary. "That was during the Depression," continues Mary. "Poor Papa, he had such a heart of gold. He'd say, 'That's OK, you don't have to pay, next week, I understand.' . . . So after going fifty-thousand dollars in debt, he had to close the store and go to work in the coal mines." (Nick Zellitti.)

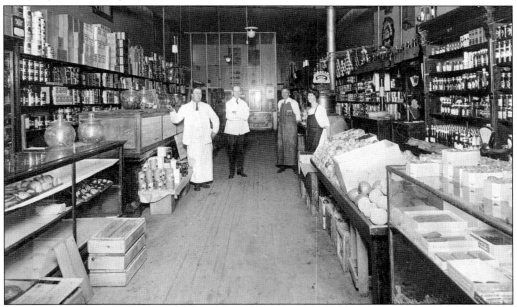

In 1923, the Mason and Ambold Grocery in the Schneider Building on Tenth Street and Main Avenue—originally established by Gus Ambold in Animas City—was operated by Walter Ambold (left), son of Gus, and Thomas Mason (third from left). Smith reported in *Rocky Mountain Boom Town* that they advertised themselves as "exclusive agents for Chase & Sanborn coffee and teas, besides offering staple and fancy groceries, meats, and bakery products." (CSWS.)

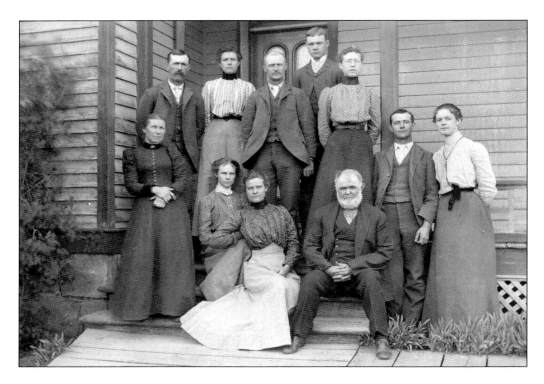

Frederick Wilson Kroeger (above, fourth from left) moved his family from north Animas Valley to Durango and purchased the G. H. Clark seed and feed store on Ninth Street, renaming it the Farmer's Supply (below), in 1921. Fred's son, Freddie (above, fifth from left) saw the business move across the railroad tracks and eventually to the site that became the south end of Town Plaza, where Kroeger's Ace Hardware is located today. In the early days, Freddie and his brothers and sisters worked at the store, selling sundry hardware items, even operating an egg processing and delivery business. Freddie (or just Fred) was a director of the First National Bank for many years, served as mayor of Durango in the mid-1950s, and was instrumental in accomplishing the move of Fort Lewis College from Hesperus to Reservoir Hill. (LPCHS.)

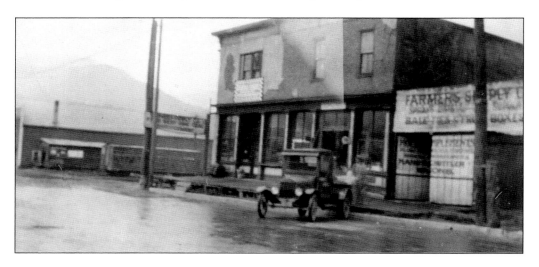

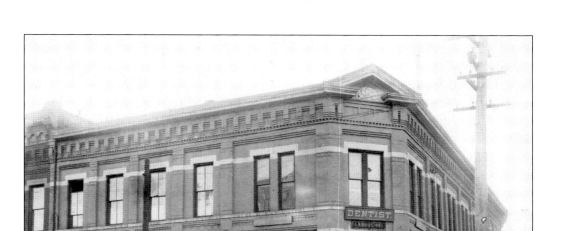

Isaac Kruschke came to Durango in 1881 from Silverton and operated a dry goods store on the corner of Ninth Street and Main Avenue, the present Gardenswartz building (above), for 40 years. A competitor with T. C. Graden, Kruschke also owned another store in Durango, the Manhattan Clothing Company. Krushke helped organize the Durango Board of Trade in 1892 and served on the board as treasurer. His wife, Hattie, was a charter member of the Reading Club. The Gardenswartz family (below) dates back to the 1880s. Lester Gardenswartz—son of Morris, who came to the area in 1906 as an investor in cattle—opened a sporting goods store in Durango just before the stock market crash of 1929. (LPCHS.)

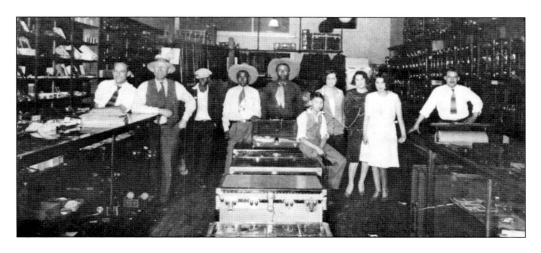

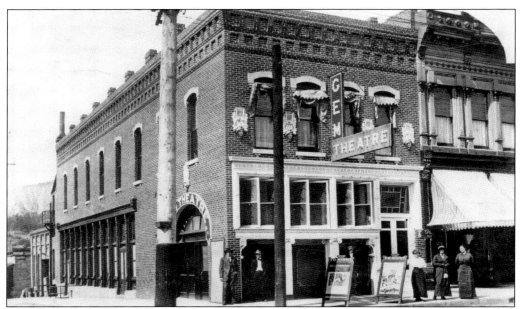

On October 7, 1915, the Gem Theatre (above)—on the corner of Tenth Street and Main Avenue—hosted a boxing match between Andy Malloy and San Luis Valley local the "Manassa Mauler," Jack Dempsey (below, right). General admission was $1; reserved seats were $2. Malloy was champion of the Rocky Mountains, and Dempsey was light-heavyweight champion of the Pacific Coast. The fight lasted 10 rounds, and although there was no decision, the *Evening Herald* declared Dempsey the unofficial winner. Dempsey went on to win the heavyweight title in 1919, successfully defending it six times until losing it to Gene Tunney in 1926. (Above, Suzie Turner Belt; below, CSWS; photograph by W. R. Rowland.)

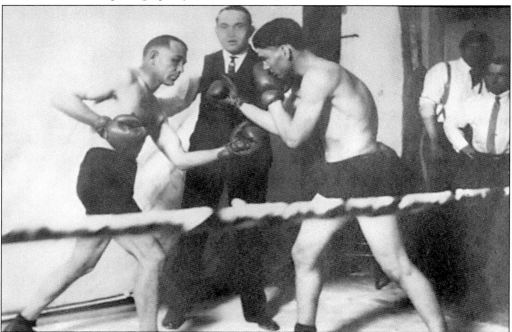

Max Baer (right), heavyweight champion in 1934, lived at 143 East Thirteenth Street in Durango, attending school at Whittier and Central. Baer's father worked for Graden Mercantile. After Baer won the championship, his boxing manners earned him the label "Madcap Maxie." In his losing match to Jimmy Braddock in 1935, as recapped in the *Los Angeles Evening Herald Express*, "Braddock was such an underdog that Baer clowned his way through—even though he was being beaten. . . . Whenever Braddock would hit him, Max would grin to ringsiders, as if it was all a lark, and he really laughed his way to defeat." During his brief reign, however, Baer was "at the top of the heap. . . . He bought 40 suits at a clip and his cars had to have 16 cylinders plus gaudy paint" (below).

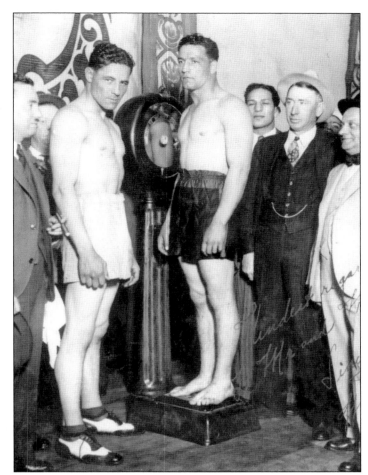

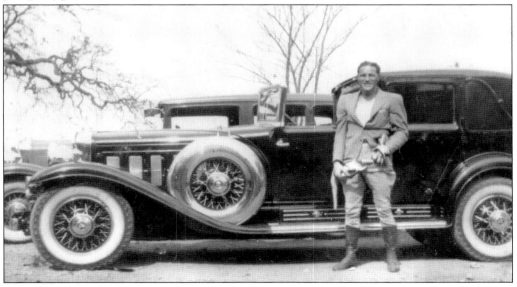

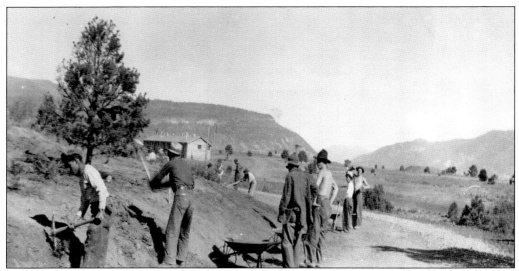

In 1933, the New Deal brought relief from the Great Depression. Government programs such as the WPA and CCC provided employment for locals, building roads, bridges, and public buildings, fighting forest fires, and planting trees (above). Men who found work in Durango were able to obtain room and board at the CCC camp on Reservoir Hill. (CSWS.)

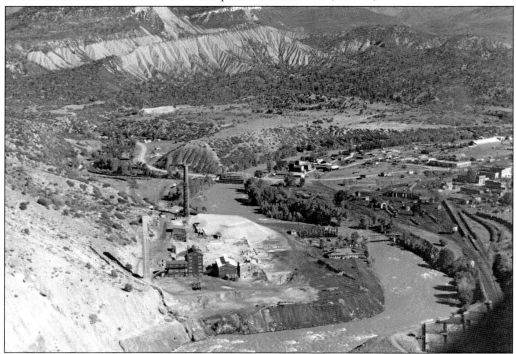

World War II brought about the opening of a mill across the river to process vanadium (above), a steel-hardening agent made from ore mined in the Dove Creek area. When the mill closed in 1945, it was learned that it had been processing uranium. In 1948, another mill went into operation to process vanadium, employing some 200 workers, and remained operating until 1963, when it moved to Shiprock, New Mexico. (CSWS; photograph by Partridge Studio.)

Six

HOLLYWOOD OF
THE ROCKIES

During the filming of *The Naked Spur* in 1953, Jimmy Stewart dedicated a monument in Fassbinder Park designating the San Juan Basin as the "Hollywood of the Rockies." According to the Durango newspapers, this monument was intended to be the first of 14, one for each movie filmed in the area in the preceding five years. Movie-making in and around Durango, however, began much earlier than 1948.

In 1917, James W. Jarvis founded the Durango Film Production Company, producing a number of shorts—including "Small Town Vamp," "Mesa Verde," and "Snow Wonderland"—as well as the first full-length movie shot in southwest Colorado, *Love of a Navajo*, which portrayed the Navajo life and customs and was set in Monument Valley. Premiering at the Gem Theatre in Durango in 1922, the movie was distributed nationwide. A major film distributor offered Jarvis $20,000 for his movie, but instead he leased the film. A Hollywood producer offered Jarvis $50,000 to make six more movies, but he decided against that, too, ending his movie-making career.

It wasn't until the 1940s and 1950s that Hollywood came calling again and movie-making in Durango boomed. Most of the early movies were Westerns, many of them featuring the Durango and Silverton Narrow-Gauge Railroad. *Ticket to Tomahawk*, for instance, was shot in the Durango area precisely because of the train. As the writer Mary Loos explained in the *Durango Herald-Democrat*, the original idea for the movie came when she and her husband, director Richard Sale, bought their first narrow-gauge model railroad engine. "Why not a story about the little narrow-gauge tracks that did so much to open up the West? . . . We did a lot of research and looked at all of the narrow gauge trains," Loos continues, "but the incredible Animas Canyon was the deciding factor to make the movie here. I'm glad because you get a beautiful look at a beautiful place that wouldn't be known without the train."

Other movies featuring the Durango and Silverton include *The Denver and Rio Grande, Viva Zapata, Around the World in Eighty Days, Night Passage, How the West Was Won, Butch Cassidy and the Sundance Kid*, and *Support Your Local Gunfighter*.

Other movies filmed in and around Durango include *Across the Wide Missouri, Lone Star, The Maverick Queen, The Cowboys, When the Legends Die, National Lampoon's Vacation*, and *City Slickers*.

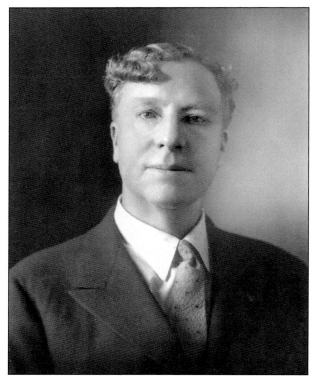

James Jarvis (left) and his wife, Ada Ferguson, moved to Durango in 1906, buying a house on Third Avenue and rearing four children there. Jarvis operated a Studebaker and Cadillac dealership in Durango for over 30 years. From 1909 to 1916, Jarvis served on the Durango City Council. Then in 1917, Jarvis founded the Durango Film Production Company and made a number of shorts, including "Small Town Vamp," "Mesa Verde," and "Snow Wonderland." "Small Town Vamp" was the first movie ever made in Durango. "Mesa Verde" was an educational film. And "Snow Wonderland" was a documentary about the train. After making the shorts, Jarvis made his full-length feature, *Love of a Navajo* (below). (Jentra Barker.)

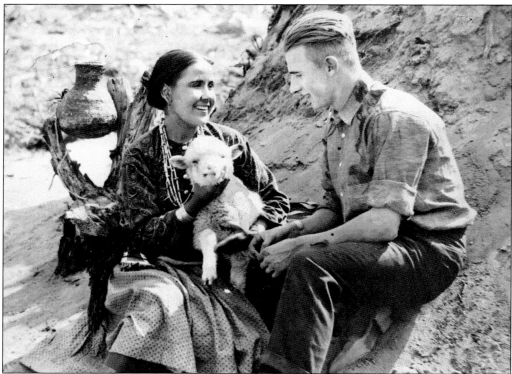

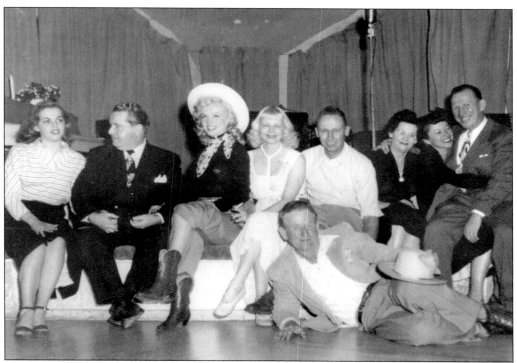

Marilyn Monroe (above, third from left) had a bit part in *Ticket to Tomahawk*, released in 1950. One day after filming, during a softball game played to raise money for Mercy Hospital, Marilyn rigged it "so her blue jeans slipped and fell to her ankles while running to first base," recalls Mary Loos. "You can imagine what happened in the bleachers when everyone saw her black lace underwear!" The real star of *Ticket to Tomahawk*, though, was the engine of the Rio Grande Southern, the *Emma Sweeney* (below). " 'She' wears big [elk] antlers across the headlight and is no movie construction job," continues Loos. "Emma Sweeney is Old Engine No. 20, a 38-ton job . . . born in 1889 in the Baldwin works and has been running ever since." (Above, Ruedi Bear; below, SJCHS.)

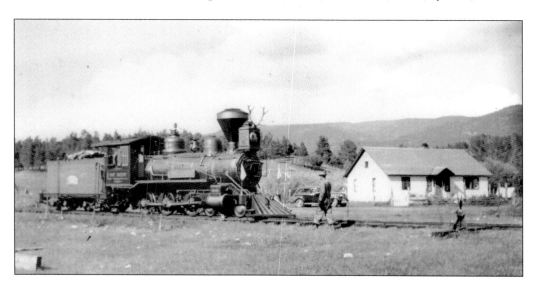

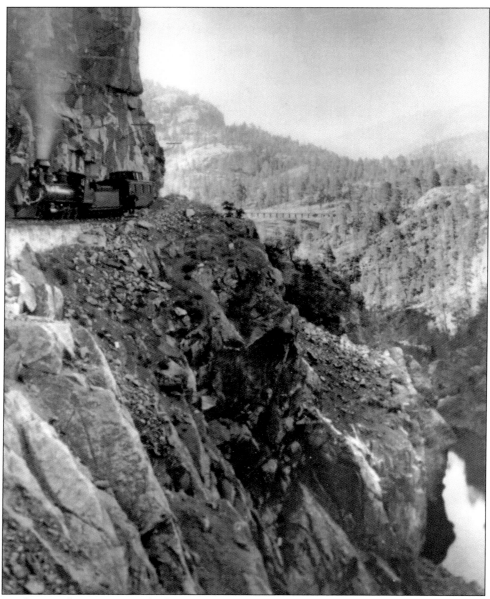

Loos also recalls a scene in which Rory Calhoun is thrown off the train and into the Animas Gorge. Although, in reality, it was a dummy that was thrown off the train, someone reported seeing a body at the bottom of the canyon. "It took the Forest Service rangers two days to pack down and find out it was a dummy," she said. Another scene took place on Reservoir Hill. Loos notes, "The crew was filming one day, and there were a couple hundred Navajos who came over as extras . . . to attack the train. Some rough horseback riding was involved, most of it bareback. The assistant director talked to the Navajos," continued Loos, "telling them that any man who fell off his horse would earn an additional $50. But 'we are Navajos,' they replied. 'We don't fall off horses.' The assistant director reminded them that they were playing Apaches in this movie—that they were dressed in Apache paint and garb. . . . At that instant every Navajo raced in front of the camera and fell off his horse." (LPCHS.)

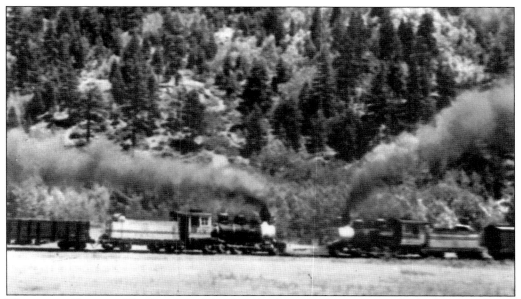

The train collision in *The Denver and Rio Grande*, shot in 1952, was not only the first ever filmed in Technicolor; it was also the first filmed in full scale rather than miniature. Although various locations were employed along the D&RG railroad line from Durango to Silverton, the climactic action takes place on a stretch of track in the Animas canyon where the Tall Timbers resort is now located. As reported in the *Durango Herald-Democrat*, "Director Byron Haskin gave the signal and . . . the trains moved forward. The engineer and fireman on each train shoved the throttles wide open and leaped. The light engines gained speed rapidly. Five Technicolor cameras mounted behind sturdy barricades picked them up as they entered the clearing and followed them across to Scrap Iron Junction."

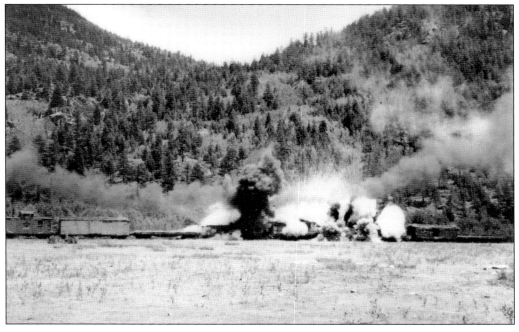

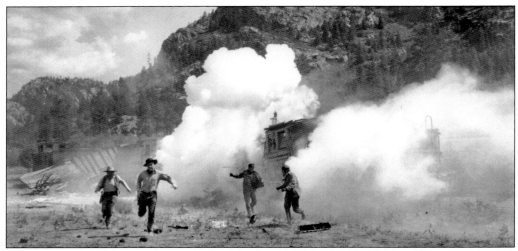

"The crash jarred the ground for several hundred yards as the roar of exploding dynamite and steam rebounded from the hiss," continues the *Herald-Democrat*. "Pieces of wood and steel shot high in the air above the smoke, sliced like shrapnel through the tops of the trees and thudded like heavy hail over the entire clearing. . . . After the explosion the roar of escaping steam was deafening. . . . Then the steam died down and the blackened remains of the two little locomotives came into view. Their boilers almost touching . . . one of the cars had buckled and splintered in every direction. Haskins gave the cameramen the signal to 'cut' and raised his clasped hands jubilantly in the sign of victory. . . . Screen stars Sterling Hayden, Dean Jagger, Edmond O'Brien [top photograph and bottom photograph, second from left], Laura Elliot and others stood chatting excitingly."

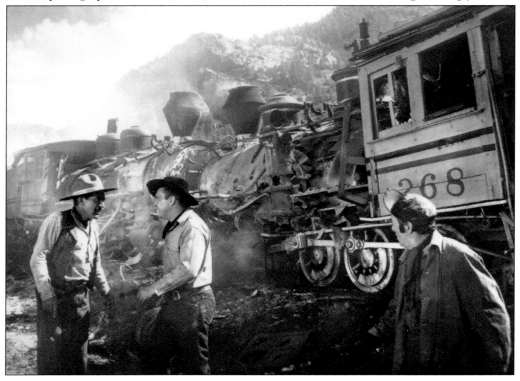

Movie-making was a unique source of revenue for Durango, often affording locals employment as extras in the films. Local cowboy Tony Herrera is seen here with Jimmy Stewart (at right, left) and Janet Leigh (below, right) during the filming of *The Naked Spur*. "How did the movies get started coming here?" "It was because of the enterprise . . . of one man—Bob Venuti," questions the local newspaper. "When Bob was the owner of 'Wilderness Trails' dude ranch . . . six or seven years ago, they entertained as guests Darryl and Virginia Zanuck. . . . As a result of Bob's eagerness about the surrounding country, the Zanucks saw a great deal of it and in the summer of 1948, Darryl sent a company here to the upper Animas valley to produce 'Sand,' the Technicolor 20th-Century-Fox picture which started the stream of companies here for movie-making." (Tony Herrera.)

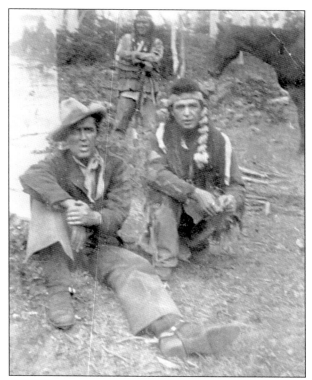

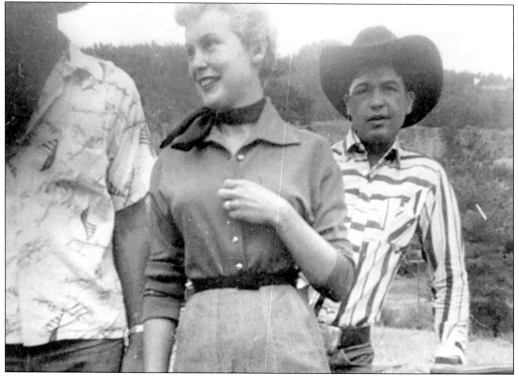

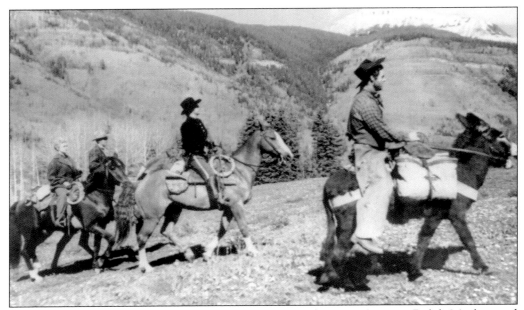

The Naked Spur—starring, from left to right, Janet Leigh, James Stewart, Ralph Meeker, and Robert Ryan—was the 14th movie filmed in and around Durango in just five years, since the first movie, *Sand*, was filmed in Durango in 1948. As reported in the *Durango Herald-Democrat* in 1952, "Five of these have been Technicolor pictures, each with a budget of over a million dollars." (LPCHS.)

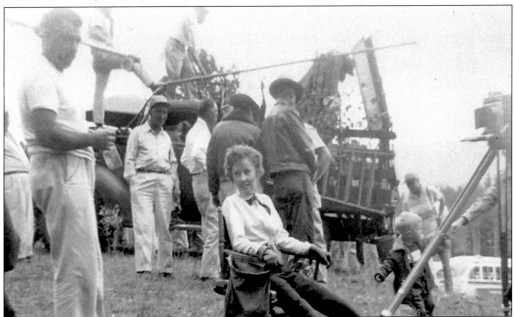

Scenes for *The Maverick Queen*—starring Barbara Stanwyck (center), Barry Sullivan, and Ernest Borgnine, among others—were shot at a deserted ranch on Highway 550, as well as on one of rancher Joe Hotter's pastures in the same area and farther up the highway on the north slope of Coalbank Hill. Town scenes were shot on Main Street and Blair Street in Silverton. (Tony Herrera.)

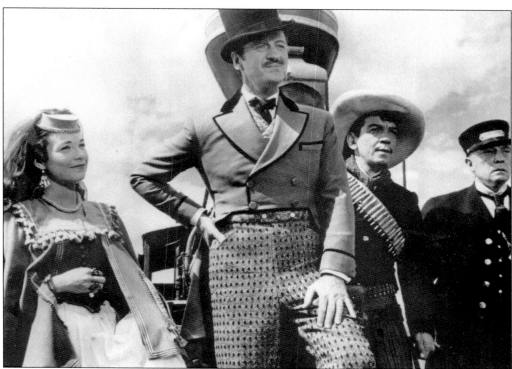

Around the World in Eighty Days—starring (above, from left to right) Shirley MacLaine, David Niven, Cantinflas, and Buster Keaton—made good use of the train. Interestingly, old engine No. 315, then out of service, was employed in one major scene. As reported in the *Herald-News*, The "315 snorts steam and smoke from a false boiler being installed in the city construction yard at Second Avenue and 15th Street. . . . A steam-making apparatus squirts the water-laden air out in the proper places. A special smoke-making apparatus is in the huge smoke stack. Both will be in operation while the . . . diesel engine . . . , camouflaged to look like a box-car, does the work of pushing the train along the track." At right, David Niven joins Col. Tim McCoy, technical advisor on the film, to survey production. (Above, Duane A. Smith; right, Tony Herrera.)

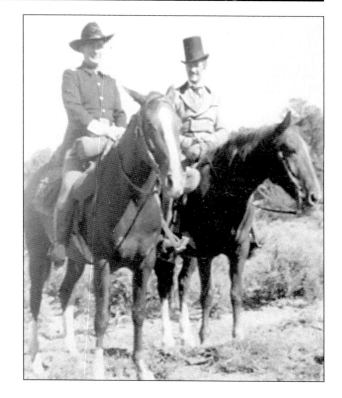

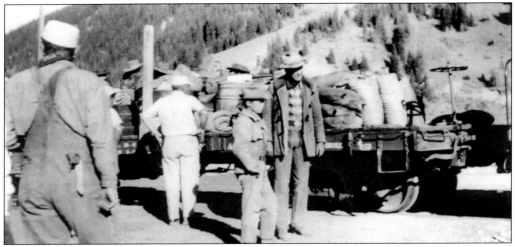

During the filming of *Night Passage*—starring Brandon de Wilde (above, third from left), James Stewart (fourth from left), Audie Murphy (below, left), Diane Foster (right), and Elaine Stewart—the spectacular Durango setting was a hit with everyone. As Foster remarks in the *Durango Herald-News*, "We're all raving about the mountains and streams, the golden aspens and vivid scrub oak . . . and of course the fishing, the hunting, the clean fresh air—and the feeling of well being that never leaves." "It's really a vacation for us," adds Murphy's wife, Pamela, who joined her husband here with her children, renting the Third Avenue home of Earl and Ventra Barker during the shoot. "When I take laundry out," said Pamela Murphy, "it's beautiful just to look around at the surrounding country." (Above, SJCHS; below, Lloyd Gladson.)

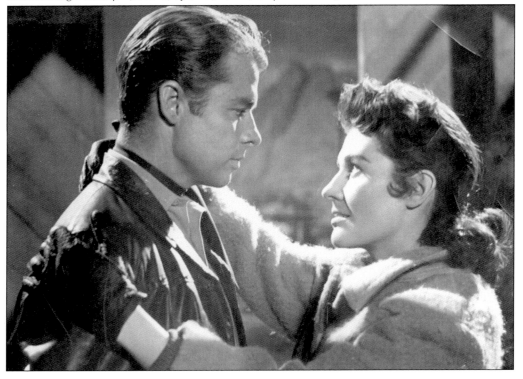

The setting caused some trouble for Elaine Stewart (at right), who was arrested for "her 'cheesecake' poses on the rocks of the Animas River," continues the *Herald News*. It seems "traffic was jamming up as drivers insisted on a bumper-to-bumper look at the free show." Judge Erwin DeLuche dismissed all charges, however, proclaiming, "Miss Stewart's charms greatly augment the natural beauty of Colorado" and that the "traffic problem is secondary." (SJCHS.)

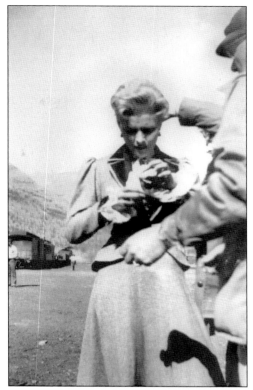

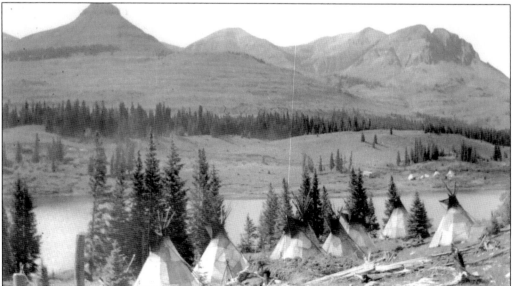

Across the Wide Missouri was also located in a spectacular setting, high in the San Juans. The *Durango Herald-Democrat* reported, "The Durango region is wild and primitive and is dotted with lakes and streams, made to order for the color cameras." For this movie, "the studio has launched the biggest outdoor building project ever, including . . . a sprawling Indian village" (shown here at Molas Lake). (SJCHS.)

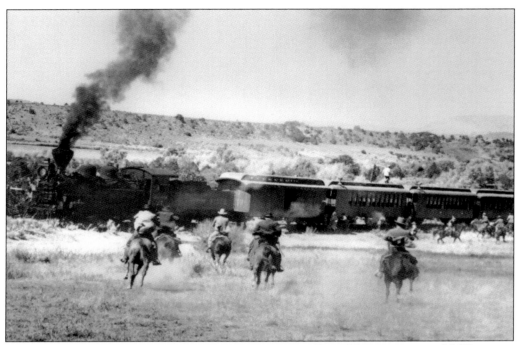

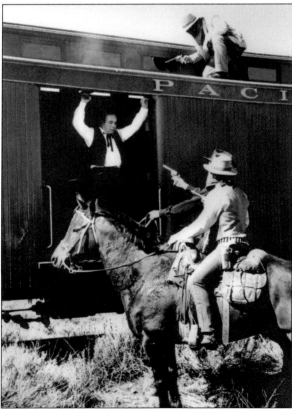

One of the most successful Westerns of all time, *Butch Cassidy and the Sundance Kid*, filmed in 1969, also takes advantage of the D&RG. As noted in the *Durango Herald*, the scene in which Butch and Sundance dynamite a boxcar and accidentally blow up the whole train—shot east of the Florida River—was a surprise for everyone, including the actors and the crew: "According to Don Demerest, who worked with movie companies on location and served as the Durango Film Commissioner from 1956 until 1986, the mail car was a movie 'extra' built of balsa wood at the roundhouse. Dollar bills were taped to the roof, and big fans were placed along the track to blow the money up in the air because the explosion wasn't expected to be very strong." (SJCHS.)

As it turned out, however, continues the *Herald*, "the special effects men laced the mail car with . . . too much powder," and pieces of the boxcar had to be collected and thrown back into the frame of the camera. In another scene shot near Durango, "Newman and Redford jump off rocks near Baker's Bridge, but in the next frame, two stunt men are sailing through the air and landing in a river in California." (SJCHS.)

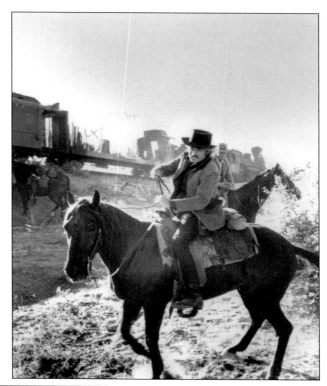

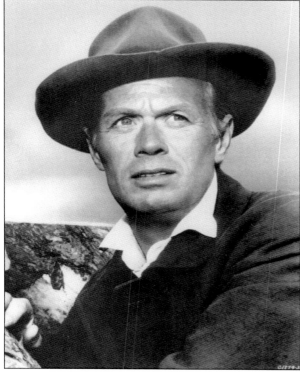

When the Legends Die—starring Richard Widmark (left) and Frederic Forrest—begins and ends on the Southern Ute reservation in Ignacio, but some scenes were shot right here in Durango. One fight scene took place at a bar called the Railroad Lounge, then located on Seventh Avenue. Another scene, also a fight scene, was set in the Rochester Hotel in a room where the kitchen is now located. (Harry Carey Jr.)

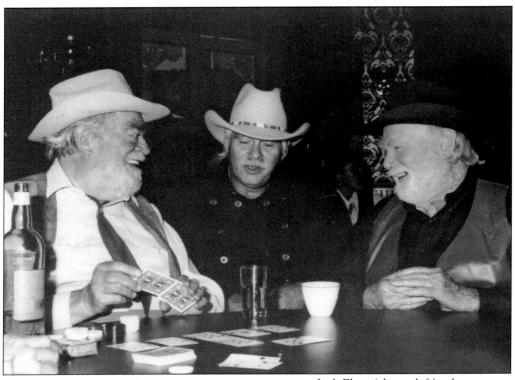

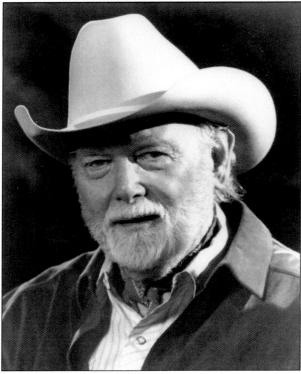

Jack Elam (above, left), who appeared in *Support Your Local Gunfighter*, would do almost anything for director Burt Kennedy, even if it meant something a little dangerous. As Elam recalls in the *Durango Herald*, "In the final scene, we had this great shot of the train in the Animas Canyon. I'm standing on the end of the train. . . . Now you have to understand that I'm scared witless of heights . . . so they have me chained to the train. This didn't help me much, until Kennedy had himself chained to me, but out of camera range." Kennedy assured Elam that if he fell, Kennedy would fall with him. Also pictured with Elam, above from left to right, are local producer Tony Schweikle and Western actor Harry Carey Jr. (Above, Tony Schweikle; left, Harry Carey Jr.)

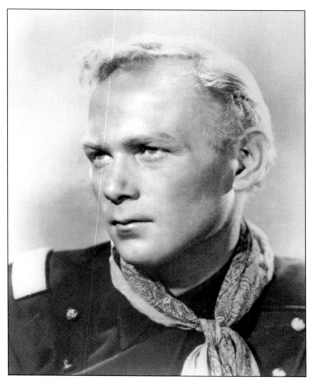

After making an appearance here at the short-lived Durango Western Film Festival (cofounded by Schweikle in 1988), Harry Carey Jr. and his wife, Marilyn, picked up from Sherman Oaks, California, a suburb near Los Angeles where Harry had lived for 70 years, and moved to Durango. When asked just why she liked moving to Durango, Marilyn Carey replies, "Because it's so different than Sherman Oaks, smaller and friendlier." Harry Carey Jr. (or "Ol' Dobe," as John Ford called him) appeared in 10 classic John Ford films made between 1948 and 1964. Three of them—*She Wore a Yellow Ribbon* (photograph at right), *The Searchers* (below, right), and *Cheyenne Autumn*—were shot in Monument Valley, Utah, just three hours west of Durango. (Harry Carey Jr.)

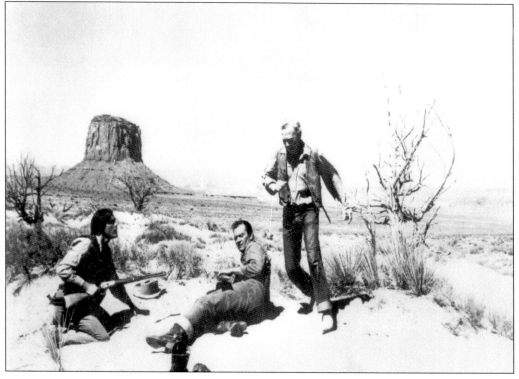

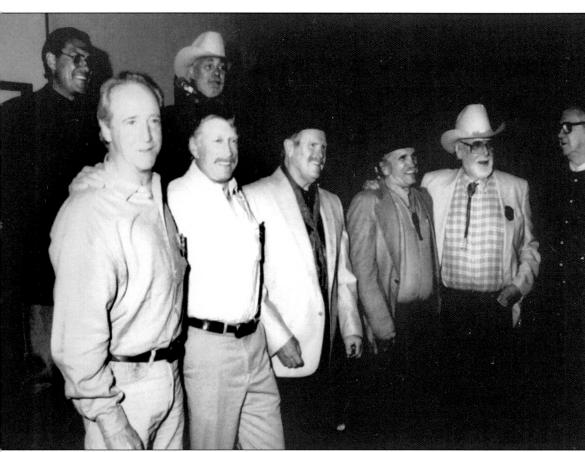

For health reasons, Harry Carey Jr. recently moved back to California, but not before founding—with Tony Schweikle (above, rear, second from left) and the author, Fred Wildfang (rear, at left)—a second Western Film Festival in 1997, which Durango hosted until 2002. Actors pictured here include Scott Wilson (front left), Alex Cord (first row, second from left), Charlie Dierkop (fourth from left), Harry Carey Jr. (fifth from left), and director Burt Kennedy (sixth from left). Durango continues to be associated with movie-making by virtue of the Durango Film Festival and the new Durango Independent Film Festival, which combined have been in business now for over eight years.

Seven

DESTINATION DURANGO

Durango is one of the few Western towns with a self-supporting downtown area still intact. Historic hotels, restaurants, and retail businesses, many in newly restored and remodeled buildings, dominate the Main Avenue Historic District. Tourism thrives in Durango. The Durango and Silverton Narrow-Gauge Railroad serves more passengers during the summer season than it ever did during the height of the old mining days. And the Durango Mountain Ski Resort brings in skiers during the winter season.

In fact, there is so much to do in Durango that it has become one of America's favorite travel destinations. Suggestions include power-shopping in Durango's chic shops, galleries, and museums; walking along the Animas River; hiking up to the Fort Lewis mesa; and checking out the Victorian homes on historic Third Avenue.

Visitors can go rafting, kayaking, and fishing on the Animas River. World-class fly fishing for trophy-size trout can be found here. Fishing, boating, water-skiing, and swimming are also available at nearby Vallecito and Navajo reservoirs.

Outdoors activities here, in the "sunbelt" of the Rockies, can be enjoyed on over 300 sunny days a year. Visit Mesa Verde National Park, 40 minutes west, or drive the San Juan Scenic Highway, traversing through some of the most spectacular country in the United States of America.

Among the many special events offered every year in Durango are the Iron Horse Bicycle Classic, the Diamond Circle Melodrama, the Wild West Rodeo, Music in the Mountains, Fiesta Days, the La Plata County Fair, the Durango Arts Festival, the Cowboy Poetry Gathering, the Snowdown Festival, the Durango Independent Film Festival, and the Bluegrass Meltdown.

As tourism grows, of course, so does the population. Now the second-largest town on Colorado's Western Slope, Durango has grown to more than 15,000 people.

The folks are friendly here and a good mix: cowboys and Native Americans, professionals and young entrepreneurs, artists and writers, and a lot of rugged outdoor types. In fact, Durango is one of the most engaging towns left in the Old West—kind of a throwback to the gentle 1960s—partly due, no doubt, to the influence of Fort Lewis College.

The history, the scenery, the climate, and the culture—all make Durango the perfect place to visit, to do business, and to live.

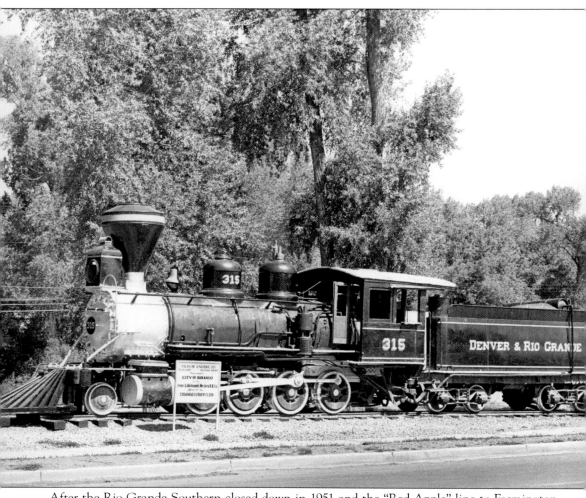

After the Rio Grande Southern closed down in 1951 and the "Red Apple" line to Farmington closed down in 1968, the Durango and Silverton Railroad became largely a tourist attraction. By the late 1970s, over 120,000 people were taking the train to Silverton. By the late 1980s, after its sale to Florida businessman Charles Bradshaw, over 177,000 people were taking the train. Bradshaw widely promoted the train as a tourist attraction and began running four trains daily during the summer and trips to the Cascade Canyon Wye and back in winter. In 1987, First American Railways, Inc., bought the train and continues to operate it to this day under the management of its chairman and chief executive officer, Allen Harper. Locomotive 315 (shown here)—built in 1895 and retired in 1949—has been recently restored and brought back into service, running on the Durango and Silverton line. Made famous by the movie *Around the World in Eighty Days*, this old D&RG Western engine was placed under the care of the Durango Railroad Historical Society for the restoration, which took over six years. (CSWS.)

Durango's first major ski area—consisting of one ski run, a toboggan slide, and a hot dog stand—opened up some 20 miles north of town in the late 1930s. A tow to the top of the ski run cost 25¢ a day for adults and 10¢ for children. In 1965, however, Purgatory had become a major ski resort in southwestern Colorado, popular with families. Recently becoming known as the Durango Mountain Resort, the ski area is now undergoing a major makeover. The new Purgatory Lodge will boast upgraded skier services, many new rental and retail outlets, and a redesigned Purgy's restaurant and day lodge. A new village center will feature an amphitheater, a water feature, and facilities for various summer activities. Current improvements include new ski and snowboard programs and a 25-percent increase in snow-making capacity. (CSWS.)

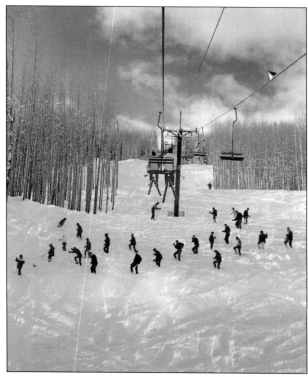

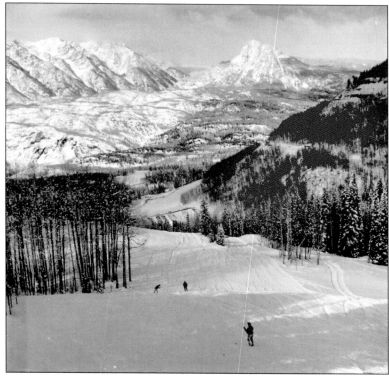

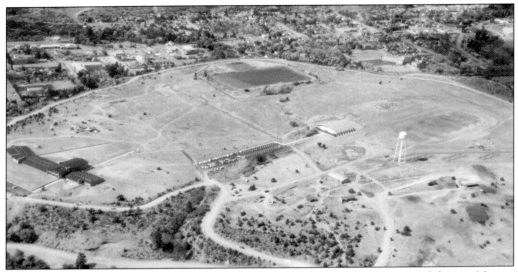

In 1910, Fort Lewis was transferred to the State of Colorado and converted from a Native American boarding school to a rural high school. In 1927, it became a junior college, granting Native Americans free tuition. In 1956, the junior college was moved to Reservoir Hill in Durango (above, Berndt Hall is at left) and, in 1962, it became a four-year college. Fort Lewis offers a fully accredited liberal arts curriculum for a diverse student population, currently numbering nearly 4,000 students. Founded by history professor Robert Delaney in 1964, the Center of Southwest Studies at Fort Lewis College (below) has become a regional center for studying and preserving the history of the Southwest. The center's new $8-million facility houses an exhibition hall, an archives library, and a special collection of rare historic textiles from Puebloan, Navajo, and Hispano weaving traditions. (CSWS.)

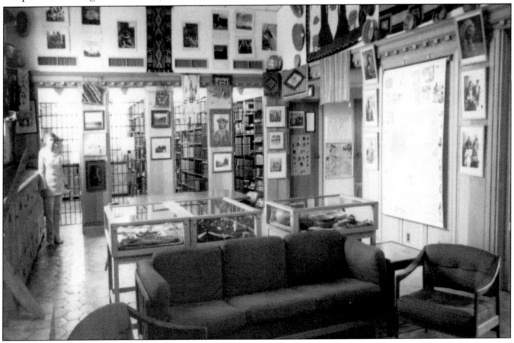

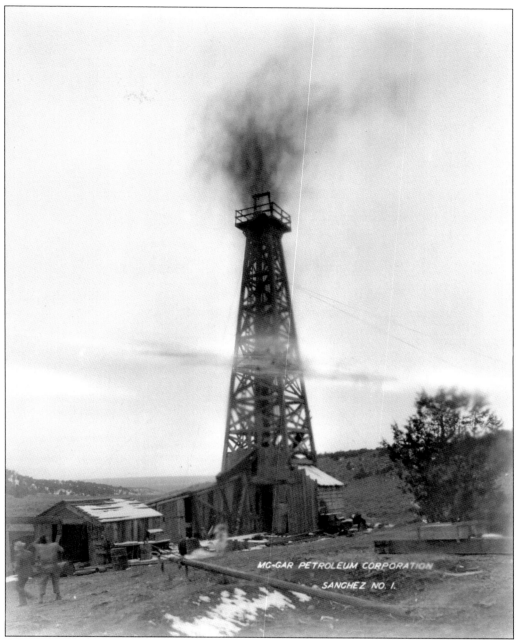

MC-GAR PETROLEUM CORPORATION
SANCHEZ NO. 1.

Oil and gas exploration first began in La Plata County in the early 1920s. Note the gusher pictured here. Natural gas was first piped into Durango from the Ute Dome near the Colorado–New Mexico state line in 1929. Natural gas exploration and development just south of Durango, however—mostly on the Southern Ute reservation around Ignacio—greatly expanded in the 1950s. Consequently, natural gas production (over $5 million worth in the 1960s) increased the assessed valuation of property in La Plata County, as well as the population. Durango alone grew from 5,887 people in 1940 to over 10,000 by 1960. Gas companies in the county still extract 35 percent of Colorado's natural gas and 2.3 percent of the nation's entire supply. (LPCHS.)

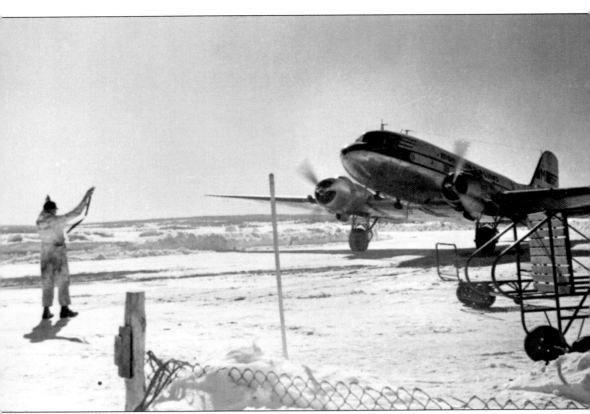

Durango's airport, which had been in service on Reservoir Hill, moved east of Florida Mesa and, in 1977, became upgraded to handle jet traffic. Featuring one of the best runways in the Four Corners—9,200 feet long and 150 feet wide—the Durango–La Plata County Airport offers daily service via United Express to Denver and US Airways to Phoenix, Arizona. The 36,500-square-foot La Plata terminal accommodates five rental-car agencies, as well as a gift shop and café. Convenient air travel service has greatly boosted tourism in Durango. Recently, AAA named Durango the third most popular destination in Colorado, trailing only Denver and Colorado Springs. (LPCHS.)

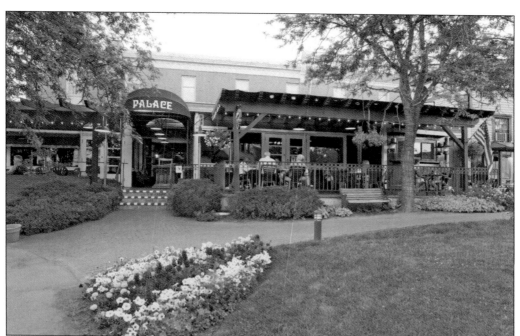

One reason Durango has become so popular is that the town has made a concerted effort to retain its historic flavor. Establishing Main Avenue on the National Register of Historic Places in 1980 has resulted in the preservation and renovation of many fine old structures in the downtown area. Even before achieving that distinction, however, private developers made attempts to recognize the historical sanctity of Durango. "Rio Grande Land," for instance—that stretch of Main south of College Street— was extensively renovated and remodeled by Jackson and Jackson Heritage Development in the late 1970s. The Palace Restaurant (above) stands adjacent to the old Palace Hotel (in background, see page 76). Rooms at the old Palace are now part of the elegant General Palmer Hotel (right), which occupies the same building as the former Savoy Hotel (see page 76). (James Jackson.)

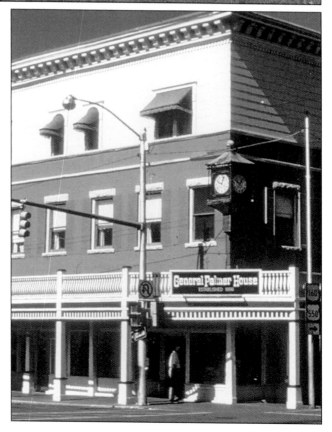

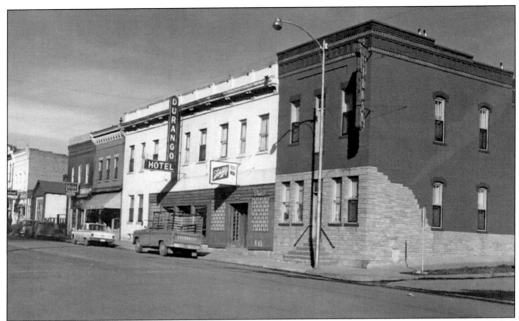

Across the street on the east side of South Main Avenue is a whole row of renovated and remodeled retail businesses, including furniture stores, clothing stores, and restaurants. On the second floor of these buildings are office suites. As shown in the 1960s before remodeling (above), the two hotels at right—formerly on the site of the old Southern Hotel and McNeely House (see page 78)—have been replaced by a parking lot. Among the historical structures still standing, however, are the buildings at 528 and 534 South Main Avenue and the N. T. Thompson building at the end of the block. (James Jackson.)

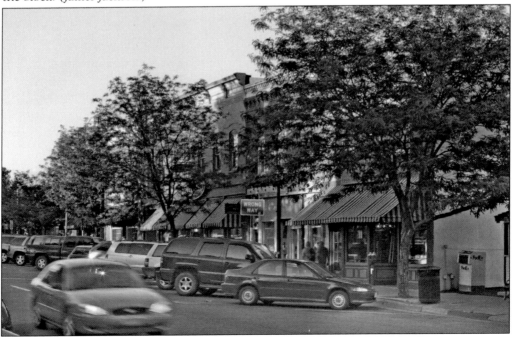

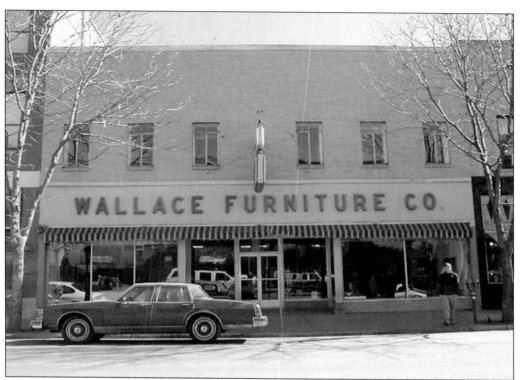

Genuine restoration efforts involve removing added-on, artificial facades, as shown here at Wallace Furniture (above), and restoring the building's original appearance as when it was Goodman's Paint and Supply (right). When finished, this Brookie Architecture restoration at 858 Main Avenue will feature retail suites on the main floor and business condominiums above. (Above, Brookie Architecture; right, LPCHS.)

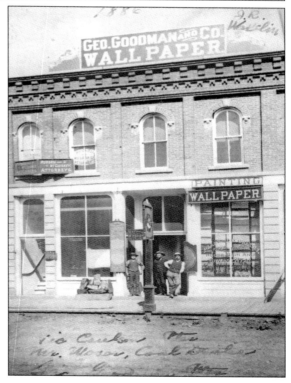

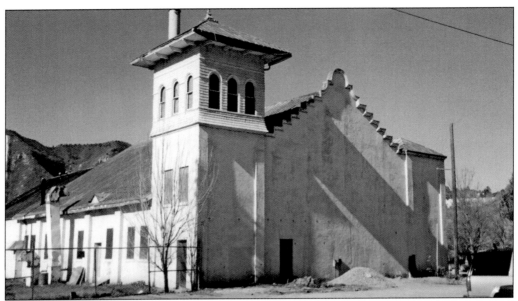

The old light and power company plant (see page 51), the earliest mission-style commercial building this side of California, has been restored and remodeled for use as the Discovery Museum of Durango. Compare and contrast the shape the building was in before restoration (above) and after (below in a photograph by Jonas Grushkin). Among its projected features are a riverfront park and restaurant as well as an interactive museum dedicated to the study of power and energy, consistent with the powerhouse building itself. (Discovery Museum.)

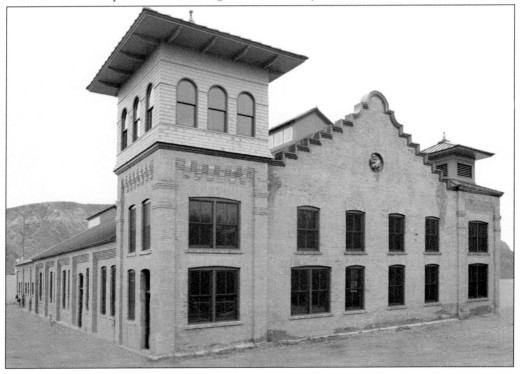

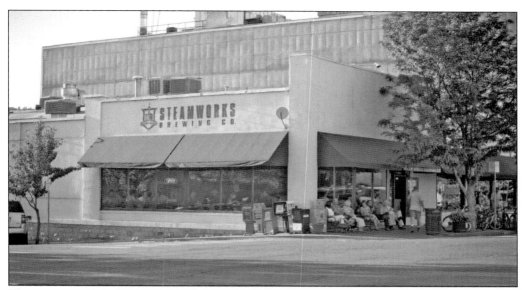

The preservation and restoration of historic buildings in Durango extended to East Second Avenue in the mid-1990s. The former home of Pat Murphy Motors at 801 East Second Avenue, built by P. W. Pittman in the 1920s, is now the Steamworks Brewery and restaurant.

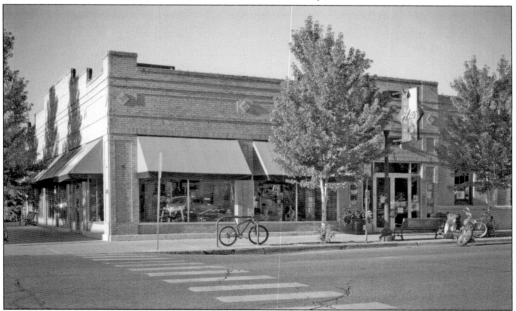

Across from Steamworks is the Durango Arts Center, the former home of the Murphy Motors garage, built in the 1930s. The 14,000-square-foot art center facility houses an exhibit gallery, a gallery shop, a dance studio, a children's museum, an art library, and the newly redesigned Diamond Circle Melodrama theater. Many of the arts activities at the center—after-school classes, the docent program, and the annual Creativity Festivity, for instance—are offered in collaboration with the Durango School District 9-R. And now, the biggest event sponsored by the center, the all-weekend arts and crafts fair extravaganza previously known as the Main Avenue Arts Festival, has moved to East Second Avenue.

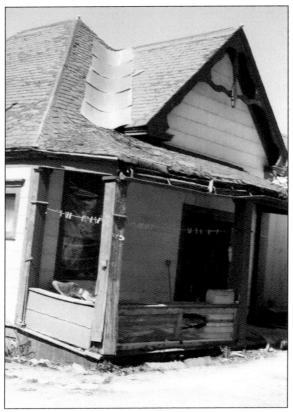

The Cyprus Café at 725 East Second Avenue—once the breakfast place of the Leland House and Rochester Hotel—was built in 1890 by T. C. Graden, one of Durango's most famous entrepreneurs. It is also associated with Balthasar "Balsey" Kern, longtime owner and operator of one of Durango's most popular saloons. Kern owned this building for 30 years. Before that, Peter Fassbinder, one of Durango's original homesteaders, and James Lutrell, Durango's first land agent, owned the property where this building now stands. When the owners of the Leland House and Rochester Hotel, Diane Wildfang and her son, Kirk Komick, applied to the state historical society for funds to restore this building, they were told "not to bother." Consequently, they restored the building at their own expense.

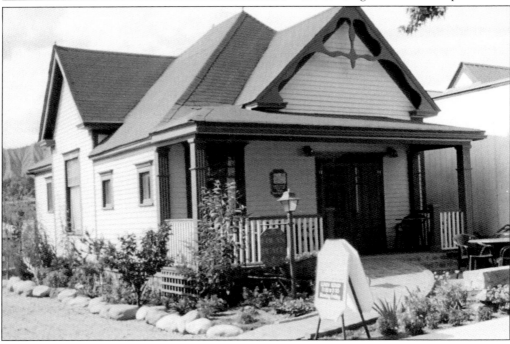

Eight

THE ROCHESTER HOTEL

The restored Rochester Hotel at 726 East Second Avenue is one of Durango's oldest hotel establishments, continuously operated as a hotel for more than 100 years.

The parcel of land upon which the Rochester now stands was first owned by ex-territorial governor and founder of the D&RG Railroad Alexander C. Hunt. The second owner of the property was Durango's first land agent, James Luttrell.

Foundations were laid for the Rochester Hotel in 1890. In 1891, construction of the building was taken over by E. T. Peeples, a local accountant and one-time county commissioner. In 1892, J. E. Schutt (president of the Schutt Mercantile Company) and W. C. Chapman (director of the Colorado State Bank, vice president of the Durango Iron Works, and a dealer in hardware) bought the property and completed construction of the building, which became known as the Peeples Hotel.

This two-story, late-19th-century, vernacular-style, brick building—originally thought to be built with about 30 rooms—was approximately 40 feet by 90 feet, with 8,000 square feet total. Flat-roofed and rectangular in shape, with a balcony in front, the building featured radiating brick lintels on all windows and doors, rough-cut stone sills on the windows, and a classic portico at the main entrance.

In 1893, the Peeples Hotel was sold to Jerry Sullivan for $6,000. The *Durango Herald* advertised the hotel as "under new management, newly furnished, excellent service, largest rooms, lowest rates." Sullivan owned the hotel for some 13 years, selling it in 1905.

From 1905 to 1920, Mary Francis Finn owned and operated the hotel, renaming it the Rochester Hotel. Mary Finn extended the front of the building to the sidewalk and added indoor bathrooms in the back.

Among subsequent owners of the hotel were Bertha M. Graden (the daughter of a pioneer farmer in the area), Edward J. Gemmill, who now lives in Denver, and Henry M. Valentine, a local property owner and former director of the Durango Chamber of Commerce.

In 1992, Diane Wildfang and her son, Kirk Komick, purchased the Rochester Hotel. Diane and Kirk completed extensive restoration work in June 1994, converting the dilapidated structure of 34 rooms and three baths into a small luxury hotel, offering 15 spacious and high-ceilinged rooms—all with full baths. The rooms in the Rochester are named after movies filmed in and around Durango. Movie posters framed in marquee lights line the halls.

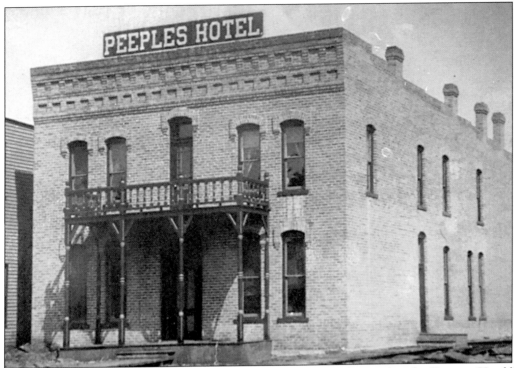

The Rochester Hotel was first known as the Peeples Hotel. As advertised in the *Durango Herald* in 1892, "Peeples Hotel offers the best of accommodations to the public." Indeed, local directories at the time listed the Peeples (along with the Grand Central and the Strater, among others) as one of the best hotels in town. (LPCHS.)

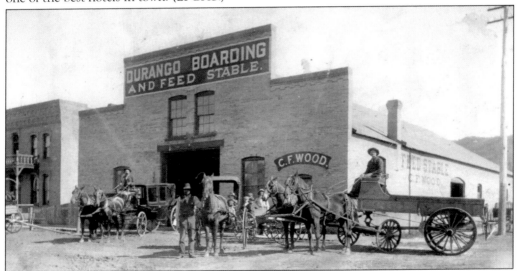

"Mrs. DeVault has the Peeples Hotel and [asks] all who want a nice quiet home to give her a call," continued the *Herald*. The hotel was situated next to C. F. Wood's stable on Second Avenue (shown here). Daily and weekend roomers found the Peeples Hotel a convenient place to stay during their visits to town. (LPCHS.)

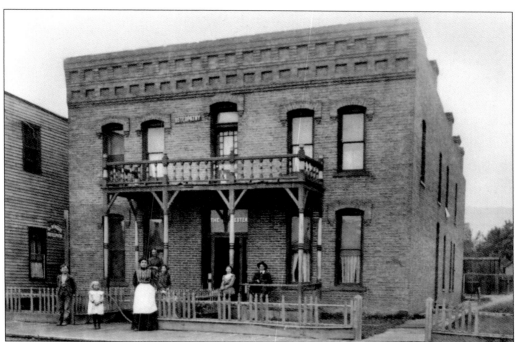

During the time Mary Francis Finn owned the hotel—from 1905 to 1920—the name was changed to the Rochester Hotel (above). Four rooms were added to the front of the building, extending it to the plank sidewalk, shown around 1908 (at right). Finn also added two bathrooms in the back. Later, sometime in the 1930s, neoclassical columns were added beneath the balcony.

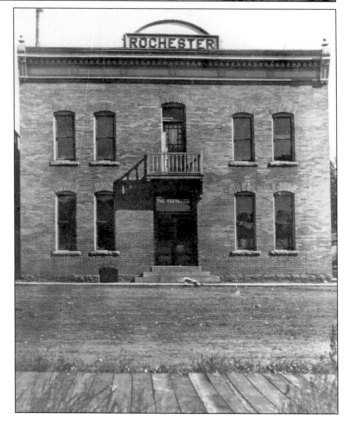

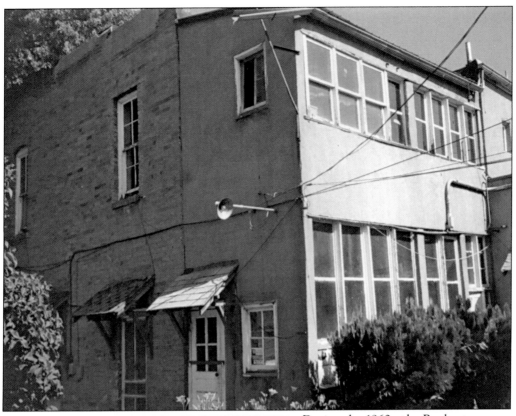

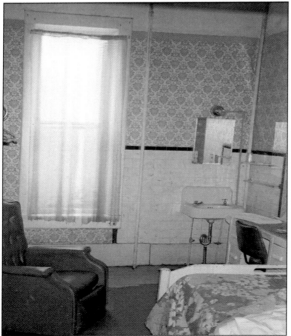

During the 1960s, the Rochester greatly deteriorated. The hotel had become a virtual "flophouse," the rooms renting for as little as $12 a night (at left). Generally speaking, the building bore an appearance befitting the burnt-out neon sign in front, reading then—with key letters missing—The "Roche" Hotel. In 1992, when Diane Wildfang and her son, Kirk Komick, purchased the Rochester, the hotel was in rough structural condition. The upper story was sagging, the floor joists were dry-rotted, and the front balcony and back porch were actually falling off the building.

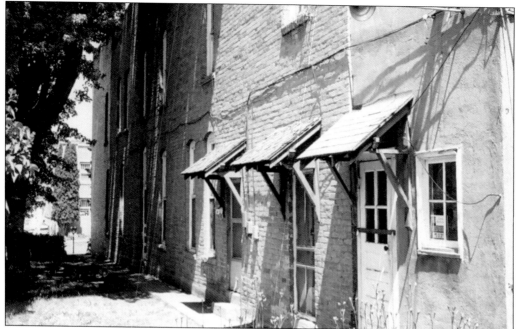

The exterior of the building was also in utter disrepair. The balcony, suffering extensive water damage, had to be completely reconstructed, securely anchored, and restored to look exactly like the original. The original portico, entablature, and parapet were also repaired and repainted. The original exterior doors were repaired and retrofitted, sanded, patched, and repainted. The original window glass in the doors was retrofitted, and the broken panes were replaced. The courtyard at the side of the building (above)—dirt-worn and littered with broken bottles and discarded cans—was paved with walks, seeded with lawn grass, and planted with flowers, ornamental bushes, and trees (below).

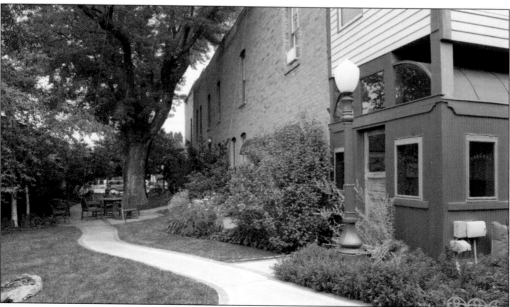

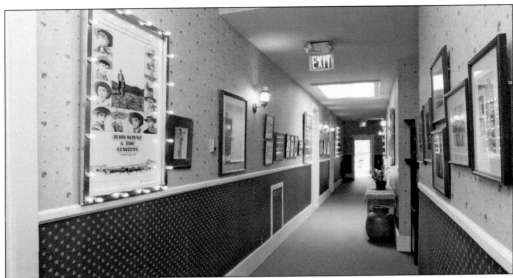

During restoration, every effort was made to retain the original appearance of this classic old building. Interior features include the original trim, hardware, doors, and windows, as well as the original skylight in the ceiling upstairs. The original interior doors and door frames were repaired, stripped, sanded, patched, and repainted and the doors retrofitted. The thresholds were replaced. The original hardware was salvaged, repaired, cleaned, and retrofitted onto the doors. Transom windows above the doors were restored—the frames stripped, sanded, patched, and repainted; the original window glass was retrofitted. Finally, a lobby was added, incorporating the original stairway with banister and balusters. A matching banister was crafted and attached to the other side of the staircase, leading to a mid-stair landing and creating an open stairwell at the side of the lobby (below).

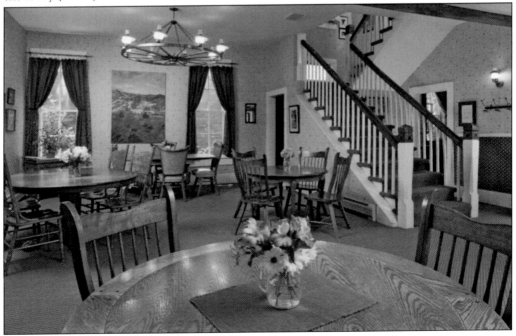

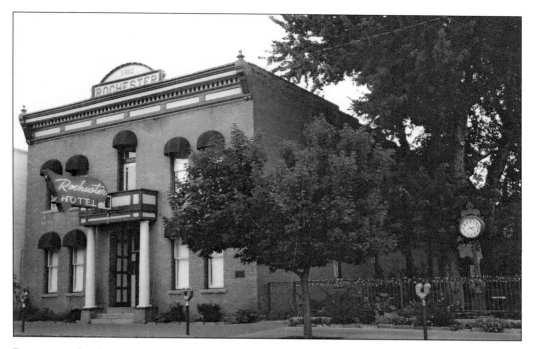

Remaining for the most part architecturally intact and standing adjacent to the Third Avenue Historic District, the new Rochester Hotel contributes to the integrity of the downtown area by helping to provide an appropriate transition between the residential Third Avenue Historic District and the commercial Main Avenue Historic District—consistent with the original intent of the town's founding fathers.

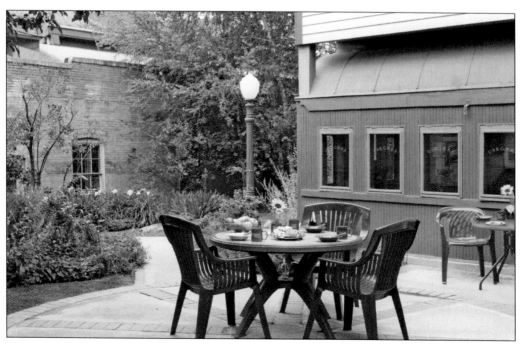

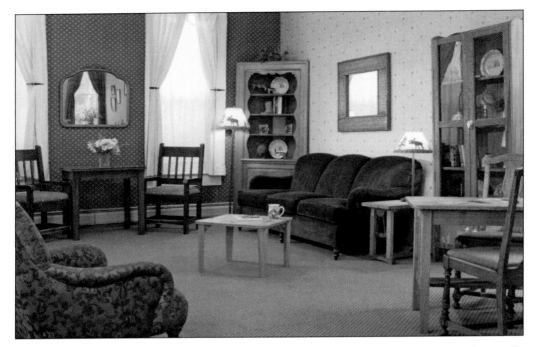

Conveniently located in a beautifully landscaped downtown setting, the Rochester is an authentically restored late-Victorian hotel, fully furnished with antiques from the period and decorated in an Old West motif inspired by the many Western movies filmed in and around Durango. The new Rochester Hotel now offers 15 spacious rooms with high ceilings and full baths. Several of the rooms are suites.

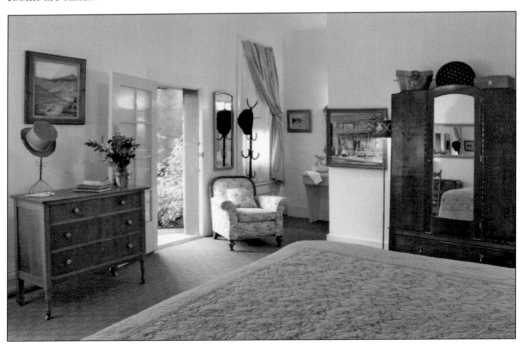

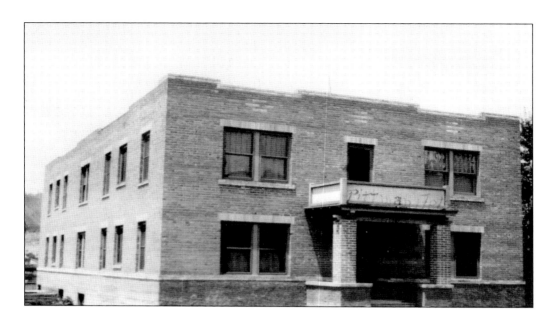

Across the street from the Rochester, the Leland House—built in 1927 by P. W. Pittman (above), longtime resident of Durango and well-known builder in the area—was also remodeled by Diane Wildfang and Kirk Komick (below). The Pittmans owned and operated this apartment house for some 22 years. Most recently, the building had been owned by the family of J. Walter Hill—specifically, his daughter Laverna Sullenberger, who was married to Robert Sullenberger, grandson of A. T. Sullenberger, the Pagosa Lumber Company magnate. (Above, Karen Pittman.)

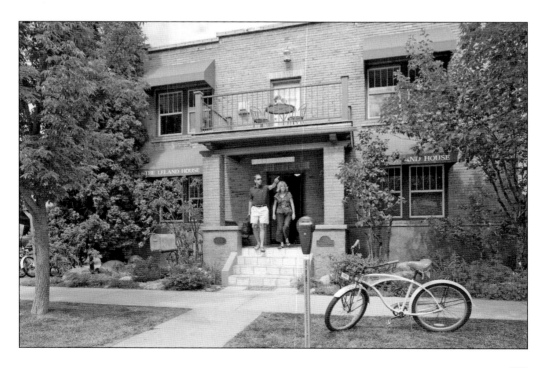

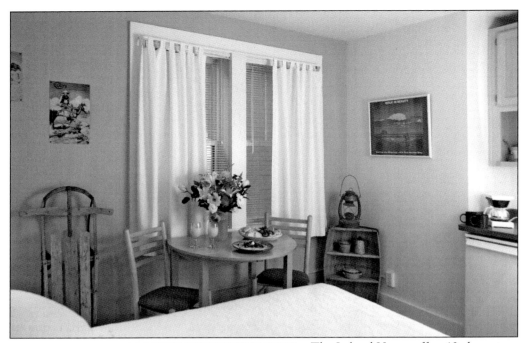

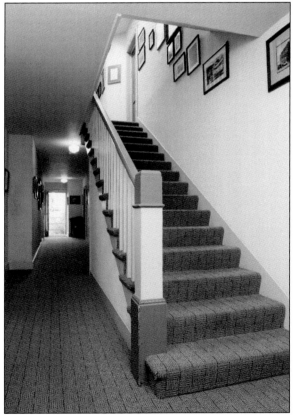

The Leland House offers 10 charming rooms, five of them three-room suites with gas fireplaces in the living rooms, and one of them a luxury five-room suite with gas fireplace and balcony. All rooms have kitchen facilities and private baths. Lining the hallways of the Leland House is a collection of over 100 historical photographs of important local figures associated with the property. Accommodations at both the Leland House and the Rochester Hotel include a complimentary gourmet breakfast featuring fresh-made scones and muffins, a selection of fresh fruit, juice, tea, coffee, and a daily entree. Afternoon refreshments are also served, featuring their famous homemade cookies.

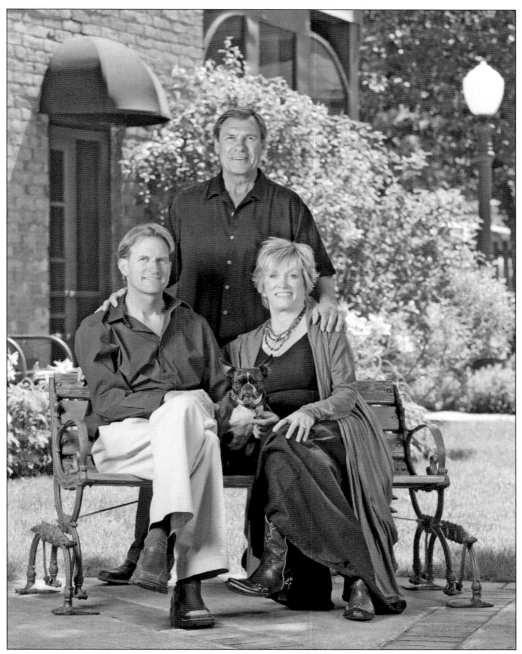

Author Fred Wildfang (standing), his wife, Diane Wildfang, and her son, Kirk Komick, owners of the Leland House and Rochester Hotel, are proud of their pioneering efforts to revitalize East Second Avenue in downtown Durango. Since their restorations and remodels at 721, 723, 725, and 726 East Second Avenue, the street has become home to chic restaurants, retail stores, a micro-brewery, and the Durango Arts Center. Because of its close proximity to Main Avenue, Second Avenue has become a popular mini-destination for visitors to Durango, as well as a "hip" gathering place for locals.

DISCOVER THOUSANDS OF LOCAL HISTORY BOOKS FEATURING MILLIONS OF VINTAGE IMAGES

Arcadia Publishing, the leading local history publisher in the United States, is committed to making history accessible and meaningful through publishing books that celebrate and preserve the heritage of America's people and places.

Find more books like this at
www.arcadiapublishing.com

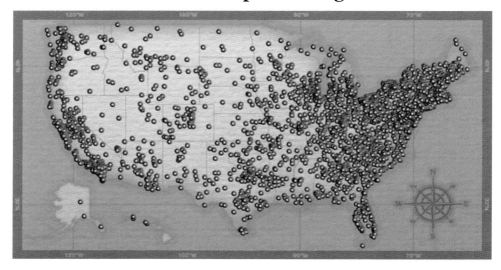

Search for your hometown history, your old stomping grounds, and even your favorite sports team.

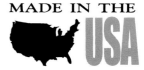